life
lessons

Contents

Introduction

This isn't a book for super-heroes.

When several colleagues and I got together to write about lessons that had changed our lives, what came out were stories of common struggles and character flaws: workaholism, rejection, doubts, fears and insecurities.

Forced – by writing a chapter – to take the long view, we came to see how God had individually met with us. We learned that none of us are doomed to spend all our lives avoiding intimacy, battling shyness, being full of our own self-importance, being insecure in God's love, or failing to trust him, for example. All of us can look back on milestones where God has met with us in our messy state and changed things. When you spend years wondering if 'becoming more Christlike' is just an empty phrase, that's a great encouragement.

We all work for a mission agency, WEC International. But every Christian has a story of a gracious Shepherd taking individual care over a wandering sheep. Whether you read this book on your own, or with a group, we hope it will encourage you in your Christian life.

Glenn Myers
Cambridge 2010

Hearts at rest

Susan Sutton

Since he looked upon me my heart is not my own. He hath run away to heaven with it.
—Samuel Rutherford

You will seek me and find me when you seek me with all your heart.
— Jeremiah 29:13

Years ago, more years than I care to count now, three friends and I declared our undying love for the most beautiful animal on earth by forming the Horse Lovers Club. We held club meetings in our back yards, read Misty of Chincoteague and The Black Stallion series, and made vows to always love horses and never shave our legs. At the same time we formed a Boy Haters Club, which was just as passionate in its intent. As the year progressed, however, so did our exceptions to the list of boys we had vowed to hate. This club eventually, and not surprisingly, folded due to lack of interest.

Over time both clubs folded. We grew out of a fascination with horses and into a fascination with boys (which led to taking back the vow to never shave our legs). To mark this passage from childhood to what we considered more mature interests, we formed a new fan club for a currently popular group, the Monkees. Throwing our pre-teen hearts just as passionately into this new club, Jane, Carol, Jenny and I faithfully read everything about Davy, Mickey, Peter and Mike. We each had our favorites (mine was Peter), memorized the lyrics to their songs as devotedly as we had formerly memorized details about horses, and imitated their weekly television show by walking with arms locked and legs crossing over each other, 'getting funniest looks from everyone we meet … hey, hey, we're the Monkees!'

Over time, this club also folded. We adored those four guys on a screen, but it was a distant adoration. There was little to keep our hearts engaged when other more immediate interests claimed our time and attention. Going the way of its predecessors, the club was fun while it lasted but faded in relevance to our lives.

The problem with clubs

Horses, boy-hating, and the Monkees had several things in common for a group of girls growing up in North Carolina in the late '60s. They engaged our hearts for a moment in time. They gave us a sense of belonging and identity. They were fan clubs and they were great fun.

I am convinced that every longing of the heart has its roots in a God-planted desire that He meant from creation to satisfy ultimately with Himself. But the world has lost its way since the creation, and right desires have gone askew. The enemy of our souls has either twisted them into wrong desires or convinced us to seek fulfillment of reasonable and good desires in wrong places. One of these God-planted desires is a longing to be part of something bigger than ourselves. We are made for something outside of ourselves, which is, of course, life with God, but because we have forgotten who we are, we look for someone else to live for and something else to satisfy us besides God.

Hearts at Rest

This may well be the reason fan clubs exist in such abundance. We long to be part of something bigger than we are and fan clubs give us a way to do this. The identification with something outside of ourselves can even influence behavior, as we proved in our Monkees imitation, a manner of walking which only besotted pre-teen girls could care to copy. Belonging to something or someone declares 'who I am' to the world at this moment in time.

The problem with clubs is that they depend on members to keep them going. This is particularly a problem for fan clubs, since fans are notoriously fickle. Horses, boy-hating, and a '60s pop group all have another thing in common for that same group of girls. They are no longer part of our lives. We grew up. We moved on to other interests. Our hearts turned elsewhere.

Hearts without an anchor

As a teenager in the '70s, the same waning interest that moved me out of a sincere devotion to horses and pop stars was at work on something much deeper than passing fads; something that touched matters of eternity rather than moments in time. I was in danger of losing my faith; at least, what faith I could claim at the time.

Church had been part of life ever since I was first entrusted to nursery helpers on Sunday mornings. I grew up knowing the lingo. I knew all of the Bible stories. This is a good thing since they are true, and I appreciate very much a childhood where church was a part of our family life. But then the teenage years hit. I began The Search for meaning and significance that happens necessarily and often painfully in adolescence.

With typical teenage angst, I wrote poems questioning the meaning of life and seriously wondered if the answer was just 'blowin' in the wind' as Bob Dylan sang so soulfully. I was, at least, blowing in the wind, drifting along on unsteady currents with no anchor to hold me down in one place. Longing to be 'myself', but not knowing who that 'self' was, I looked to my friends to determine who I should be and how I should act. Since they were drifting along in their own currents of uncertainty and insecurities, this was not helpful. Adolescents do not make steady anchors for each other.

'Who am I?' 'Why am I here?' 'What is the world all about?' were questions of the heart and mind that we were all flinging to the stars.

During this period of questioning, I never thought to look to the church for answers. God was already part of my life. I had 'been there – done that' and was still doing it as far as attendance goes. Infant-baptized, Sunday School taught, and youth group regular, I had the religious side of life figured out. Or so I thought.

What I didn't know at the time was that although church was part of my life, God Himself was not, at least not in the way He intends to be. An actual relationship with God was at the time as non-existent as a relationship with my favorite of the Monkees. The distantly adored Peter was just an image on a screen and a face in a magazine. At least in his case, I had a picture in mind when I thought of him. I had no idea what God looked like. He was as impersonal as a character in a book, to be believed in, respected and adored, but not known.

Thinking I had all that was possibly available in the God department, I never reached out to Him to fill the longings of my searching heart.

'Deep calls to deep' says the psalmist . . .

Thankfully, He reached out to me.

Life with a capital L

In my sixteenth year something happened that changed me and is changing me still. I fell in love. It was an engagement of the heart so deep and real that it ended The Search, and connected my heart to the Jesus I had heard about every week for most of my childhood but had never met personally until that sixteenth year. He moved from a character in a book to a living person I could know.

'Ha!' you say, 'I knew it. Of course.' Well, I didn't know it. There was no 'of course' in my teenage heart when the connection happened. I was clueless that knowing God up close and personal and that a relationship with Him was the key to finding everything my heart longed for.

I remember well the place and time that everything changed and Life with a capital L began. The seed of this change was planted by a new group I had joined in high school called Young Life. Yet another club. The difference was that its leaders were college students who obviously had not grown out of their heart engagement. In fact, they seemed to be growing more and more into it. They were downright passionate about Christ who was the focus of the club. They were passionate enough to travel thirty minutes every week from a major state university to a rural high school and spend time with a group of adolescents drifting along in our various currents. To our parents, Young Life was a wholesome group that meant evenings they didn't have to worry about what we were up to. But to us it was an ocean that all of our unanchored hearts longed to moved towards, because we saw in the Young Life leaders something greater and more real than we had in our own lives.

During the course of that year, I watched the leaders. To them it was serious stuff to be a Christian. Following Christ went beyond the walls of church. Their God-connection spilled over into the days of the week beyond Sundays. They spoke as if they knew God and He touched every part of their lives.

Hmmm, I thought. I should be more serious about my faith. After all, I am a Christian; I should start acting like one. So I did. I carried my Bible around and even began to read it outside of Young Life meetings. I joined a prayer group. I joined a Bible study. I paid more attention in church. I worked on being friendlier, not just to my friends but to everyone.

It was behavior modification at its best and it was a miserable year. Outwardly I looked pretty good by stepping up Christian behavior, but inwardly the restlessness remained. In fact, it not only remained but grew. Dissatisfaction with what I saw in the world, which began The Search, deepened to dissatisfaction with what I saw in myself. Maybe, I thought, the world isn't the problem. Trying to do the things that a good Christian should do only made me keenly aware that I was not a good Christian. I was not the loving, caring, patient, spiritual person that I hoped others saw on the outside, and I had an increasing sense that God saw through the image I was trying to project.

He did see through, of course. The One who sees everything knows what is in the heart He created. I now realize that it was God's determined love and infinite grace that allowed the growing internal dissatisfaction. He had something to tell me so He brought me to a place where I was ready to hear it. The spiritual place where The Search would end and Life would begin was honesty with myself and with God about the real me in contrast to the outward, visible 'me' as a Christian in high school. In other words, I had to find my spiritual red dot.

'You are here'

Lao-Tzu, a Chinese philosopher who lived in the sixth century B.C., wrote, 'A journey of a thousand miles begins with a single step.' A modern day rendition is written on a T-shirt that I have from the Colorado seminar on spiritual formation with Larry Crabb. The T-shirt reads in bold lettering, 'Every journey begins with a red dot.' Dr. Crabb's point is that we need to know where we are before we can get to where we want to be.

This is certainly true in a day and age of mega-conference centers and mega-malls. A red dot is an extremely important part of a map. Whether I am attending a conference and trying to locate a seminar room or trying to find a store in an unfamiliar mall, I head for a map. The first thing I look for is the location on the map of where I want to be. Once I find the seminar room or store, I look for the red dot that says 'You are here.' I cannot reach where I want to go in the vast labyrinth of a mega-mall unless I know two locations, where I want to be and where I am. Both are necessary for the journey.

In the same way, to move forward in life with God we need to locate our spiritual 'red dot,' that place of soul-honesty that says, 'Here I am, God.' He knows, of course, where we are. Doubting, hurting, angry, confused, afraid, prideful, struggling with an area of sin. Our true state of heart and mind may be hidden from those around us, but not from God. And yet we are afraid to be honest with Him.

I sometimes wonder what would have happened if Adam and Eve had been honest with God at their point of failure, if instead of hiding from Him they had run to Him as the One who knew them completely, which included a potential for wrong choices, but also loved them completely. If they had not covered up their true selves but had told God everything that happened including their doubts of His word and lack of trust in His love, I believe the conversation would have been different. God is the safest place we can go with our true selves, because He knows us more than anyone else can ever know us. Yet we continue the enemy's lie that He cannot be believed or trusted. Instead of being real, we cover-up not only with each other but with God, as Adam and Eve tried in the garden.

I was about to meet with the real God, not as a distant figure of Sunday school lessons and ideals to emulate but as He is, the living God who created me for life with Him. I was to learn that the real God wants the real me. He is not interested in outward shows of behavior and activities but in inward connections of the heart.

What happens when the real you meets the real God? Real transformation.

The heart finds its way home

The physical place where God brought me was Windy Gap, a Young Life retreat center in the mountains of North Carolina.

A Young Life retreat means days of exhausting fun (keeping all those hormones at bay) and nights of spiritual challenge. Saturday evening was the main message for the weekend. A hundred plus students packed into the Windy Gap conference room heard a compelling message of God's love, of Christ's sacrifice on the cross and of His right to our lives. At the end of the message, we were encouraged to reflect on what we had just heard. The message hit home for me and I wanted to be alone, so I moved outside the conference hall, found a rock beside a small stream, and sat down.

I had never heard so clearly and personally what God in His love had done for me. His *ahab* (pursuing love) had to open my eyes before I could see that I was made for something more and that all my questions found their answers in Him. His *hesed* (merciful and compassionate) love had to do something about the sin that kept me disconnected from my source of true Life. Both of these aspects of divine love, God's passionate commitment to us and His compassionate mercy towards us, are seen most clearly in Christ on the cross.

Everything within me knew that this was true, but I also knew that I was trying to live the Christian life and it wasn't working. Selfishness, criticism, pride, insecurities and concern for the approval of others still ran rampant in my life. With the message of God's love and of the cross ringing in my ears, and with a desperation to be free of my 'self' that was not what I wanted it to be, I cried out to God, 'I've tried! I can't live the Christian life. I can't be good enough. I can't do this!'

Deep Truth responded to deep honesty with these words: Good, I've been waiting for you to come to this point. Now we can begin.

Using words from the message, the Holy Spirit wove Truth into my heart.

I know you can't. That's why I came. That's why there is the cross. Now stop trying to do it on your own and start living Life as it is meant to be lived; My Life in you and through you. Surrender your life to Me, and let's live this Life together. Let Me introduce myself. I am Jesus and I am the One your heart is searching for.

The proverbial light bulb turned on. I saw that what was missing in my life was Christ Himself. I had, in fact, been living Christianity without Christ. My efforts were sincere. God truly was becoming more important to me and living for Him was increasingly a desire of my heart, but even in my stepped-up version of Christianity, Jesus remained a distant figure whom I was trying to emulate. The 'red dot' reality was that I was still the star of my own show, so to speak. Life was still about me:

Me trying to be a good person.

Me trying to be a better Christian.

Me trying to 'live for God.'

There was, in fact, a great deal of 'me' in my life and little of Christ Himself. I understood now that it was meant to be the other way around.

That night I talked with God. It was not the first time that I had prayed, but it was the night that prayer moved from ritual to conversation. It was the night that Eternity stepped once more into time and God through His son, Jesus, reclaimed a soul that was made for Him and stilled the restless heart of a teenage girl sitting on a rock by a stream on a mountain.

The universe settled into place and I felt as if I had come home. In fact, I had come home to Someone. The One who created me, died for me, loved me for myself and sought me for Himself now welcomed me into His embrace.

Some would say that I accepted Christ into my life for the first time that night. Others would declare that the Jesus I had believed in as Savior now became my Lord. Both of these are true. The living Christ did enter my life when I understood that being a Christian is not my attempt to live the Christian life but Christ Himself living in and through me, doing what I cannot do on my own. Christ also became at that point a Lord to follow rather than an ideal to emulate. But I say that deeper things happened when the real me met the real God. A member of a club became a member of a family. An image-projector became an image-bearer. A restless heart found its anchor. A soul found its way home.

Over thirty years later, I can say unwaveringly that Jesus' words that night have proven true. Going through life with Christ is an engagement of the heart so strong that I have never grown out of it. In fact, like those Young Life leaders, I have grown into it more and more because love, if it is genuine, only matures as the years go on. God's passionate and pursuing love for us, shown clearly in Jesus, is the most genuine love the world will ever know. Christ at work in us and through us is the greatest hope the world will ever know.

Susan Sutton is from North Carolina. Along with her husband Louis, she served 13 years in Chad planting churches among Muslims through medical and educational ministries. They are currently Directors of the WEC USA Sending Base.

She has published:

A Quiet Center: A Woman's Guide to Resting in God's Presence (1999)

A Sure Path: Going Forward with Christ When We'd Rather Settle Down in the World (2003)

A Vision of the Deep: Discovering the Treasure of Life in Christ (2009) (this chapter is an excerpt from that book)

For Discussion

See that your chief study be about your heart:
That there God's image may be planted;
That there His interests be advanced;
That there the world and flesh are subdued;

That there the love of every sin is cast out;
That there the love of holiness grows. – Jonathan Edwards

God looked into my heart as a teenager and knew all that was in it. This is not surprising.

- The heart is designed for God: Ecclesiastes 3:11, Deuteronomy 5:7; 30:15-20 Isaiah 43:7, 21
- The heart reveals who we are: I Samuel 16:7, I Chronicles 28:9 II Chronicles 6:28-31

- The heart is God's focus for change: Jeremiah 24:7 Ezekiel 11:19-20, Jeremiah 32:38-39 Ezekiel 36:24-28
- How do you feel about God knowing everything that is on your heart at any moment? How honest do you feel you can be with God? With others?
- The red dot on a map says 'You are here.' What is your spiritual and emotional 'red dot' in reference to life with God?

Spend time with God telling Him honestly where you are at this moment in life and in your walk with Him.

The point of no return

Evan Davies

New Zealand is a beautiful country full of mountains and green valleys. There are lovely beaches, fjords, alpine peaks and a spread of climate from sub-tropical to near-Antarctic conditions. The people are friendly and the population of four million extends throughout cities, country towns and farming villages.

I was just 21 years old and sitting in the home of a dear friend in the city of Hamilton. For three years I had the privilege of living in New Zealand working first as a salesman in a Christian bookshop and then in a furniture store. A group of young people had come together for one of our regular meetings. I had been adopted by this team who were being mentored by a godly older couple and encouraged to reach out to children and restless young people on the streets. Today it was going to be changed; instead of a message from our leader we were going to listen to a tape recording of an Argentinan evangelist. It was going to be something very different for me because I wasn't really sure what I wanted to do with my life. I was facing inner battles and also the bigger questions of life choices. Should I settle down in New Zealand, get a good job, buy a house, keep in touch with a church but basically choose to go my own way? Or was there another way?

I knew that I was a Christian. My parents had been powerful illustrations of love towards God and living by faith when they followed God's call to go to Congo as missionaries. As a little boy I can remember my father explaining the basics of God's love to me and then I had the childhood memory of kneeling down in the bathroom of my grandmother's home in Wales asking Jesus into my heart. As I grew up in a missionary children's home in Scotland, I knew that I loved God and that I wanted to know him better but I really wasn't sure that I was a Christian. Every time I went to our local church fellowship and I heard again the gospel story explained I wondered if I was fully in God's family like my parents and the people who had the closest impact on me. Taking the opportunity with a friend to go through to Glasgow to attend a week of Billy Graham meetings, I finally came through to an understanding of the truth of John 1:12 with a real certainty that God had accepted me for Jesus' sake and that I was now a full and definite member of his family. It was settled.

My parents and two younger sisters had come home from Congo after seven years away. When I had completed school four years later, they decided that I should join them as they moved to New Zealand where they were to take over WEC mission representation. The idea was that I would be able to live with them making up for some of the years of separation. But it was not to be, for there was no immediate room for me in the Auckland accommodation with which they had been kindly provided. The result was that I ended up in Hamilton with the Winger family and was introduced to their extended network of keen Christian young people.

As we listened to the recorded message, God started speaking to me. The Latin American evangelist was sharing some thoughts from 2 Kings 7 specifically focusing on the four men with leprosy who deliberately tried to find food even if they died in the attempt.

The Point of no Return

The challenge to me centred round the thought, 'Are you willing to run risks for God – even to gamble with your life if need be?' Just like a pilot has to judge 'the point of no return' and know that beyond it he has to keep flying to his destination rather than abort the flight, so I needed to decide whether to go on with God and obey him regardless of the consequences. It pulled me up short, for I had secretly thought that if the going got tough as I followed God, I could choose to settle on the certainty that I was a Christian but plan to take a lower easier path. Quietly while I listened a battle raged inside me. Was I willing to hand over the reins of the rest of my life and say 'Lord, take me from now on. Everything I have is yours. I want your way only and the decision to obey you is made for ever. This is the point of no return and there is no turning back.' I agreed and prayed the prayer.

For weeks I told nobody, but I knew that a major turning point had been reached. It was my agreement with God and nobody else. Before long the issue was being challenged. After a move to Auckland, I heard that my friends in Hamilton had been abundantly blessed through a new move of the Holy Spirit and I was concerned and cautious. Was this of God or just a human thing? As I prayed about it I had the encouragement from John 14, 15 and 16 that the Spirit had been given to glorify Jesus and if I wanted the same, I would come to no harm. A visit soon after resulted in all my fears being demolished and my life touched to overflowing by the Holy Spirit. Jesus became more than a name but a central reality in my life.

With a life for God ahead of me, I realised that I had the opportunity to follow a definite career path. I wanted to go into teaching but I had the feeling that God was speaking to me about formal Bible training. Sensing that this was God at work, I went back to the decision reached in Hamilton and said, 'Lord, I am available for your will.' It was now a matter of following the gentle nudges of the Spirit, saying 'no' to one direction and 'yes' to another. By the middle of June 1961 I was studying at the WEC Missionary Training

College in Tasmania, Australia, where I faced a whole new series of disciplines as I was learning in God's school. The Bible became more precious and understandable than ever before. I started grasping the truths of what being united with Jesus really meant. Prayer in faith was demonstrated in front of my eyes as we prayed for God's provision for College needs. Old inner battles were being dealt with and I enjoyed a new walk of confidence in God. The question now was 'What next?'

I had two alternatives in mind: one, a mission field and the other, returning as a staff member to the home where I had been brought up. Godly people advised me that I was on the wrong track and again I said 'Yes Lord, I'll do what you want.' Before long the Principal of the Missionary Training College approached me about joining their staff team and I felt a growing conviction that this was what God was saying. About the same time God started speaking to me about one of the lady students and in an amazing way she was also approached by the staff before we had expressed our real feelings for each other. It's a long story but the outcome was that Jenny and I knew this was a divine direction and a happy one for us both. Obeying God had led to the best outcome and cleared the ground of all confusing steps. When we got married we felt so strongly about this that we asked the cake decorator to write the words 'GOD FIRST' on our wedding cake so that all could see we meant business for life.

As time went on at College, we faced numbers of choices and impossible challenges but always for me life was undergirded by the already settled 'point of no return'. Whatever God wanted was what I was willing for. We didn't have pots of money, sometimes we sailed close to the wind, but God kept meeting our needs. Every six or seven years we had the privilege of taking time out of the college programme and travelling overseas to visit graduates at their places of ministry and to see where the needs were greatest. It was uncanny: when we had to travel our income suddenly rose and when we came back it reduced to a settled lower figure even though we made it our policy never to ask for help.

The Point of no Return

As the years went past God showed me that there were many times in the Bible that his children had to reach something like a point of no return. I remembered Moses at the Red Sea – people all around asking what they should do, the Egyptian army behind pounding along in hot pursuit and the waters of the sea in front. Gideon was faced with leadership of Israel even though he regarded himself as insignificant and inadequate and his enemies as strong and well equipped. The youthful David had to walk towards the giant Goliath with only his simple weapons and his experiences as a shepherd of God's faithfulness to him. Isaiah responded to God's call even though he felt so unworthy. In spite of his youth and helplessness Jeremiah fulfilled the call to prophet ministry. The disciples had to take the broken bread in their hands and go towards the 5,000 people when Jesus ordered them. Peter let go of the side of the boat and walked on the water in response to Jesus' command. Paul 'was not disobedient to the heavenly vision' even though everywhere he went he was warned that prison and hardships faced him. It was evidently a biblical principle and in fact all those who have been given new life through the death and resurrection of Jesus are duty bound to live for him whatever the cost.

In 1978 Jenny and I were appointed to the role of principals of the college. This took us into a new stage of challenge and responsibility. Before long we were faced with a dilemma – how to handle an older student couple who seemed intent on defying my leadership. Many new leaders have to deal with the uncomfortable realities of going from being people-pleasers to sitting in the hot seat and having to make unpopular decisions. It was good to have a supportive and frank team who gave good advice, but in the end I had to work through the implications and do what was right. I came back to my bedrock position of dependence on the Lord and called on him to make very clear if this situation was as serious as it appeared. I needed his finger to point out the correct path. Within a short time we had an early morning visit from another student. That led to crystal-clear information that confirmed the situation was indeed as serious as we suspected and clarified our need to act. When confronted the couple were shocked but in the end seemed relieved and I knew that God had given me confidence to do what was right.

The relentless cycle of college life was intense. There were times when pressures of trying to fit everything into the curriculum, the need to be fresh for a lecture or chapel session, end-of-term interviews, business decisions, public ministry, finding new staff and juggling rosters all conspired to put me under stress. I am not naturally a person who shrugs off tension easily and I was prone to migraines. But I knew God had led clearly and I could not turn back from his call. One of the most crucial realisations I came to understand as foundational in my Christian walk was that all the members of the Trinity were with me all the time. Jesus – all of Jesus – was living in me and I had access to his power, grace, peace, resilience, holiness and coping ability. As I had handed over all the reins of my life to God for ever, He had committed all of himself to me and I had access to his immensity. This was how I learned to cope in daily life.

Jenny and I loved being on staff in Tasmania. Over 27 years we made so many friends in the state and community; the staff were wonderful to work with; students in their hundreds were coming in and moving through out to fruitful ministries all round the world; we were blessed in our teaching, practical and pastoral roles; and God had given us two lovely children whose lives were at crucial stages of training and moving into career paths. But then in February 1990 twice I heard the still small voice of God hinting that this period of our lives was coming to an end. I did not share this with Jenny at this stage as I sensed this would be a huge step for her. We were soon to leave on a nine-month sabbatical round the world and I prayed that God would show us his will. I was still committed to living out that Hamilton promise. After travelling to Asia and the Middle East we arrived in Germany for a two-week holiday in St Georgen in the Black Forest. One night Jenny woke to hear the Lord speaking to her that our time in Tasmania was coming to an end and that God had another plan for us in the International Office of WEC. She felt it was so ridiculous that she didn't tell me.

We went on to Scotland where we were planning to attend WEC's 1990 International Conference. It was good and we were blessed at the interaction with others of our peers and the challenges coming through the various sessions. As the three weeks came to an end Dieter Kuhl, WEC's International Secretary at the time, mentioned to us that he was seriously thinking of asking us to work alongside him as Deputy International Secretaries, but he needed to clarify something else first. With that surprising suggestion ringing in our ears and hearing what God had been saying to us individually, we left for a three-month visit to Brazil. During our time in that awesome country we had some great experiences and also opportunities to speak at different meetings. One day after sharing through translation with a group of women at a large Baptist church, the pastor's sister approached us. She said that she had a message from God for us but wondered if we wanted to hear it. We both said we would love to know what it was. Interestingly this was all taking place via translation from Portuguese to our Dutch co-worker who translated it into English and back again. The message she had for us was that even though she did not know us, God was saying that the work we had been in had been very fruitful but that was now finished and God was opening a new door before us that would be more fruitful and far-reaching. We were amazed that we would come half-way around the world to be given such a clear word from God.

After Brazil we moved to the US where we enjoyed fellowship with WEC members, visited various colleges and received the formal invitation to join the International Office staff in England. We shared the news of the invitation with our Tasmanian college colleagues and our children and received their approval. Jenny still was not fully at peace because she was not sure she could do this new job. She only came to a settled conclusion when we were attending a Bible study in Los Angeles where one of the members spoke up and said he had a message from God in Psalm 73:23-26 for somebody present who was fearful of the unknown. That afternoon we wrote accepting the invitation.

Before long we were back in Tasmania where we faced our final year and the handover. As the day came closer for the conference, which was to choose our replacements, I had been having big doubts. Were we making a big mistake? Would we be happy in our new job? I didn't say anything to Jenny knowing she had already faced this battle. However on the very morning of the meeting we received in the post a small letter written three weeks before from the lady who had given us God's message in Brazil. On a card inside were only written the words of Isaiah 7:9b 'If you do not stand firm in your faith you will not stand at all'. It was like an arrow to my heart. Back again I went to the promise of 1961 – just trust the Lord and obey him. He knew what was best. To cap it off another letter came also that same day from our good friend Helga Meinel with the words of 1 John 2:3-6. The 'point of no return' was the safe route and we could face the International Office confident that it was God who was in charge and would lead us.

The twelve years based in the International Office stretched and opened us to the full dimensions of WEC work around the world. It was no picnic for there were many letters to write, people to talk with, problems to resolve, changes to embrace, climates and cultures to cope with, pastoral issues to carry and administration to oversee. Yet, meeting God's servants as we travelled round the fields and sending bases and taking part in many conferences was not boring, for we were able to see at firsthand the fruits of missionary endeavour, meet many Missionary Training College graduates, and share in the challenges of the future. As an international team also we had to walk carefully together with God and to realise that open fellowship and regular prayer were fundamental if the work was to be carried out for God's glory. For me it was not to be insisting on 'my way' but God's way just like he and I had agreed upon in Hamilton those many years before.

The Point of no Return

Even after stepping out of the International Director's chair and moving into 'retirement' God still calls me to follow his leading. A visit to the college in Tasmania awakened a burden to see the team encouraged and given 'hands on' help. Jenny and I said to WEC leadership that we would be willing to help for a month or two to tide them over a shortage of staff. The answer came back that we were needed for a year. From long experience we knew that being involved again in the college would stretch us in all kinds of ways. Were we really willing for this? Was I willing for this? Some time later I was sitting in a church in Adelaide listening to the message given by the senior pastor and I sensed again the voice of God speaking to me. 'Yes, I want you to go to Tasmania for a year.' Suddenly it was as if I was back in New Zealand those many years ago and looking afresh at the contract I had made with God. For me the issue had been settled long ago. If God wanted me to go I would go. It was quite a challenge for us both, we were getting older, the college had changed a lot over the 16 years since we had handed over leadership and there were staff shortages and some big decisions to be made. Wonderfully God spoke peace to our hearts in the early months there and day after day he gave us encouraging and promise-filled verses. As we faced the new responsibility it was much bigger than we had thought and we felt really s-t-r-e-t-c-h-e-d but the assurance was there, God had led and he was able to help us cope. By the end of the year, there were new staff members on site and new leadership, big decisions had been made and the future was positive.

So for our lives the motto was still the same 'JESUS FIRST' and the words of the East African revival song were true.

'I have decided to follow Jesus,
I have decided to follow Jesus,
I have decided to follow Jesus,
No turning back,
No turning back.

Life Lessons

'Though none go with me, yet still I'll follow,
Though none go with me, yet still I'll follow,
Though none go with me, yet still I'll follow,
No turning back,
No turning back.'

Evan Davies is the son of missionary parents in the Congo, taught on staff at WEC's Missionary Training College in Tasmania, Australia and was a member of WEC's International Office. He has co-authored Meeting Jesus in Australia *with Judy Raymo (1991) and* Straight from the heart: What keeps WEC going and growing *with Stewart Dinnen (2004).*

For discussion

1. Does Evan Davies' story make you anxious? Why or why not?

2. Put into your own words what 'the point of no return' is all about. Find some examples in scripture (or look up the ones Evan summarises).

3. Are you 'past the point of no return' in your walk with God?

Rejection, resentment and self-pity: transforming the mind

Jean Goodenough

Why does God call Christians to become missionaries in other countries? 'To spread the gospel' is the response that most often comes to mind. But many missionaries could give a second reason: because sometimes it is the only way to bring to light things in their lives that need to be dealt with.

I was one week away from my 21st birthday when my minister announced from the pulpit that I had heard God's call to be a missionary. While others searched for months or years for 'open doors', I had casually walked through an open door, only to hear it slam shut behind me. And was that a key that I heard turning in the lock?

God had called me and He was making sure that I did not back out. Eight years later I arrived in the Ivory Coast. The first six months were relatively easy, consisting of three months orientation and three months helping a Swiss missionary as she taught the Bible in local primary schools. It was only when I settled in one place to do language study that three buried issues very slowly started to work their way to the surface. Eventually all three would come to the surface together and God would deal with them in a single day.

I guess we all have expectations, both positive and negative, based on everything that we have previously experienced. We rarely think about them until something happens to challenge them. Before going to Africa I had been a nurse. As a nurse I was either on duty or off duty. When on duty all my attention had to go to my work, at the beck and call of patients as well as routine tasks. But the moment I left the ward my time was my own: I could eat, sleep, read, go out, do whatever I liked.

Even at Missionary Training College where free time was short and precious (the Sabbath day of rest was a standing joke) we were normally free on a Saturday afternoon. That was our time, our off duty. And on Sunday morning we could lie-in for half an hour or so.

I carried this clear-cut concept of on- and off-duty with me to the Ivory Coast. As I settled into my new home, living with senior missionary Olive Howard, I began to realise that there was virtually no on- and off-duty, not even a lie-in. Every morning at 5.30 the pastor rang the bell for prayers. These prayer times provided spiritual food for the local Christians who were unable to read the Bible themselves. Everyone assumed that missionaries would attend unless they were sick. The only chance for a lie-in was on the rare occasion when it rained in the morning and the prayer bell was not rung. As the weeks turned into months the incessant routine made me more and more tired. Eventually my weariness prompted the older missionaries to decide that we would all benefit from a regular weekly lie-in so we took it in turns to miss prayers.

Having days off was another problem area for me. Personally I believe God's plan for people is to rest one day in seven. This rarely happened. I was reminded of the feeding of the five thousand (Mark 6:30-44). In that story Jesus first says to His disciples, 'Come with me . . . and get some rest,' then spends all day preaching to a vast crowd and finally says to the disciples, 'give them something to eat.' Some rest that was! In Africa we seemed to exist in a constant 'feeding of the five thousand' situation. Time after time my colleagues planned to have a day off at home. Then someone came to the door asking for advice, or wanting them to act as an unpaid chauffeur. The day off evaporated.

I don't think the older missionaries made a conscious decision to ignore the Sabbath and certainly God wants us to be prepared to meet unexpected needs. However, the fact that unexpected needs seemed to crop up almost every week led to time off being a rarity. The only way for us to enjoy a real day off was to get into the car and drive forty miles to the nearest big town where there was a swimming pool. But that was not possible every week. During my first four-year term of service we did well if we went to the pool once in three months.

(Following our home leave, Olive and I were more successful in having days off, scheduling them into our weekly timetable. If there were too many interruptions we felt free to take more time on another day. It also helped when the Krieg family moved to another town which had a lovely swimming pool. Once a month we visited them and enjoyed a refreshing swim.)

But during that first year with Olive I found myself living a tightrope existence where I was rarely able to unwind. Constant demands led to a build-up of resentment and self-pity. My feelings were deeply buried. I never confessed them to God or to my colleagues. I do not recall even acknowledging them to myself. Eventually they revealed themselves in physical symptoms. For a year I suffered from low-level nausea almost every day. A medical examination showed that my duodenum was inflamed. Although I was relieved to know my symptoms were not imaginary and thankful that the condition cleared with medical treatment, I knew from my nursing experience that the root cause probably lay in my mind and spirit rather than in my body.

In those days new workers went through a probationary period of one to two years after arriving on the field and before being accepted as full missionaries during the annual field conference. I was somewhat disappointed not to come up for acceptance at my second conference, some eighteen months after I arrived but knew that I would certainly be considered at my third conference. Shortly before we were due to leave for conference, Olive told me that Wolfgang and Hanni Krieg wanted to discuss something with me. Having been uncomfortably aware for some time that all was not well with my spirit I felt quite nervous as I sat with Olive in the Kriegs' living room.

First, Wolfgang pointed out that as a young missionary who had not yet finished my 'probation', I was still teachable. He said that sadly many missionaries became considerably less teachable as time went by so he wanted to point out a failing while I was still willing to learn and to do something about it.

Wolfgang's challenge certainly wasn't anything that I anticipated. He told me that I was failing to greet visitors properly and that I had a tendency to withdraw even when the visitors were fellow missionaries. I had the habit of excusing myself and going off to my room halfway through the evening. At first I could not understand how this could be a failing. It had never occurred to me that I might be missed if I withdrew from a group of missionaries. Nor had it ever entered my head that any of them might want or need my company. Wolfgang then recommended that when I went to conference I should seek counsel from Betty Nowland, a missionary who had recently returned to the field after a long absence and who had a deliverance ministry. Because I did not know her and was uneasy about anything that might be demonic, I felt considerable apprehension about our impending encounter.

I need not have worried. To my great relief Betty was a gentle, non-threatening person. With sympathetic probing she led me to talk about myself, especially my schooldays.

I told her that when I was at grammar school I had been largely ignored by my class mates. No-one sought me out to be their friend. Being poor at games did not help – I was always the last one chosen for a team. By the time I reached the fourth form I was resigned to spending my morning break and dinner hour alone. At the same time I was missing a lot of schooling because I was terrified of my German mistress. Headaches or stomach aches were frequent and very convenient! Returning to school after one such absence, I was stunned when one group of girls invited me to join them at break. Nor was it a one-off invitation. The girls accepted me as part of their group and even invited me out after school. Eventually curiosity prompted me to ask one of them why they had included me in their group. Pauline explained that one day when I was absent our form mistress had challenged the class to be more friendly towards me. Her group had heeded Miss Jones' suggestion and remained friendly until we went our separate ways on leaving school.

I was deeply grateful for Miss Jones' intervention on my behalf and the friendship of those girls prevented me from being a total misfit in society. By the time I lived in the nurses' home with other student nurses I was no longer the odd one out. I did not analyse my assumptions, but deep down took it for granted that if I had friends it was because people were deliberately trying to be kind to me. I never dreamt anyone outside my own family could love me and want me for myself.

As we talked, it became clear to Betty that habits and assumptions formed in my teens had persisted right through my life. When I was converted I suddenly had a whole new circle of friends, people who were on the same spiritual wavelength as I was. (In this sense I was better off than some new Christians for whom conversion means losing old friends.) I never consciously thought, 'These people are just putting up with me and loving me because they are Christians,' but it was there just the same. Now, in my early thirties, this deeply buried assumption was producing fruit that was being noticed by others.

'I think we are dealing with a spirit of rejection here, Jean,' said Betty. To this day I do not know if her diagnosis of 'a spirit of rejection' referred to an evil spirit that was oppressing me, or to an attitude of mind learned over many years of feeling rejected. Or maybe it was a combination of spiritual deceit and oppression on top of human rejection. Whatever it was, it had messed up my life and relationships and I didn't want it around any more. Betty prayed for me. Then I prayed, renouncing the 'spirit of rejection'. It could be said that the spirit of rejection came from outside and I was a victim of it. But as I prayed, the Lord clearly showed me that resentment and self-pity were also having a very unhealthy effect on my life. So I renounced them, too.

Betty said, 'When you renounced these things it was like sawing through a tree. The separation has been made, but the trunk is still standing and needs to be pushed off its roots.' At her suggestion, I took a daily stand against all three evils. Every morning I declared, 'In the name of Jesus I renounce the spirit of rejection, resentment and self-pity.' Then, because I did not want to leave the house 'swept clean and put in order' but unoccupied (Matthew 12:43-45), I added, 'And I accept the fruit of the Spirit: love, joy, peace, long-suffering, gentleness, goodness, faithfulness, meekness and self control.'

Initially I was most conscious of the battle with the unholy alliance of self-pity and resentment. Every time I felt one or the other arising I renounced it in the name of Jesus. As I became less moody so I was easier to live with. Olive no longer had to face stony silences over the dinner table! The main battle lasted six months, during which I routinely renounced rejection, resentment and self-pity in my morning quiet time. Eventually I stopped while on holiday – a time I didn't feel at all sorry for myself. However, I have never stopped asking God to fill me with His Spirit each day so that I can have the His fruit in my life.

Of course there were ups and downs, but I was aware who my enemy was. One incident is especially vivid. It was a Sunday. I had attended the local church while Olive went out of town to a village church. As usual I arrived home first and decided to tackle the washing up. I had been washing up quite happily and was starting to wipe when a little voice whispered, 'How come it is always you who has to do the washing up?'

Rejection, Resentment and Self-pity

Before I knew what was happening I was feeling sorry for myself and somewhat resentful. Then another little voice whispered: 'Hey, you were perfectly happy a few minutes ago. That wasn't your thought. It came from outside.'

'What a dirty trick!' I thought, 'Resentment tried to sneak in at the backdoor and pretend it had a rightful place in my heart.'

'I renounce the spirit of resentment and self-pity!' I announced. When they seemed reluctant to leave, I threw down the tea towel, marched into my bedroom and came out with my cassette player. Putting on 'Scripture in Song' it was not long before I found myself praising the Lord. By the time Olive came home, the washing up was finished, the kitchen was tidy and I was able to greet her cheerfully.

This incident taught me an important lesson: resentment and praise are like darkness and light. They don't mix. I cannot recall when I started to record my thank-you prayers, but it has developed into a regular part of my quiet time. Every morning I write down five things for which to thank the Lord. I have thanked Him for all kinds of things, from the beauty of creation to the fact that I slept well. I have thanked Him for salvation and thanked Him for exciting holidays. I have thanked Him for good health and for dentists. I have often thanked Him for reminding me where something was that I had mislaid.

Thanking God for five things every morning makes me more likely to thank Him for all kinds of little things at other times of the day. If I am dragging a load of shopping uphill I can thank Him for shopping trolleys and that this is giving me a workout. Sometimes I thank Him that it isn't raining. When it is raining I think of something else, 'Thank you Father, it's not cold and windy.' And when cold rain is blowing straight into my face, I say, 'Thank you Father that there's no ice on the pavement.'

Perhaps because the nature of rejection was different, I did not have the same kind of spiritual battles with it. Rather I had a sense of release, mixed with growing wonder at the knowledge that people might actually enjoy my company and want to be with me. It was a totally new idea and made a huge difference to my life. Working from the new assumption that people liked me unless there was very clear evidence to the contrary (usually there wasn't) I was able to be more at ease with them. I no longer spent ages analysing every personal comment for negative connotations or signs that the other person intended to hurt me. I was able to accept that even comments which did hurt me were probably not intended to, enabling me to forget them quickly and not brood over them.

At one point the Lord permitted me to see rejection from the another perspective. We were visiting some workers from another mission in a nearby town. One worker greeted us warmly. Her colleague came in, greeted us briefly and then disappeared to her room. We were surprised and somewhat disappointed because we had looked forward to seeing her, too.

The first missionary shrugged apologetically. 'She's like that sometimes.'

Suddenly I saw that this poor lady was behaving in exactly the same way that I had done. She probably had no idea that she had left disappointed visitors or that they would have valued her company. How many people had I hurt by behaving that way? How often had the spirit of rejection caused me to reject others without even being aware of what I was doing? That brief incident taught me a lot, including the fact that I was not unique in suffering the consequences of rejection. Out of it has come a deeper awareness of other people's needs and that God can use me to meet those needs.

The deliverance from rejection, resentment and self pity proved to be such a life-changing experience that I rate it second only to new birth in Christ. It is possible that the main reason that God sent me to Africa was to bring these things to the surface so He could deal with them. Sometimes I speculate what I would be like if He had not stepped in to change my attitudes. I am sure that I would have few friends. It is exhausting to be friendly with someone who is supersensitive, resentful and always feels sorry for herself.

After almost four years in Africa I returned to England for a year's home leave. I already felt like a different person. But God wanted to make sure that I had really got the message that people loved and accepted me. He wanted to take away even the remaining scars on my wounded, rejected spirit and once again He used others to do that.

Part of my home leave was spent speaking at meetings and representing WEC. At one convention I helped to staff the WEC stand and got to know other Christian workers in the exhibition tent. During the week God used two of them in a lovely way to show me how much I was accepted. One worker approached me at lunchtime and asked, 'Can I sit next to the happiest missionary I know?' And when I was saying goodbye at the end of the week another missionary gave me a big hug saying, 'I've really appreciated having you around.'

If that was not enough, a few weeks later, I was at a local ladies' meeting that I attended whenever I was free. I enjoyed it because it was a place where I could be 'me' rather than 'the missionary'. One girl, who had missed the meeting the previous week, suddenly said to me, 'Oh, were you here last week? If I had known I would have come too!'

Jean Goodenough served the Lord for six years in Africa and then returned to the UK. She had great fun as the 'voice of WEC' when working as a receptionist at Bulstrode, WEC's UK headquarters. Later, the Lord had to speak to her through three different people before she accepted that He wanted her to edit the Worldwide magazine. At the time of writing she is the Prayer Mobiliser for the Basque people and would love to hear from you if you think God might be calling you to pray for the Basques!

For discussion

1. Jean's story shows (a) a decisive break with attitudes from the past and (b) a daily discipline to transform the mind and heart. Explore in the scriptures the themes of:

- Confessing your sins to one another and praying for one another.
- Transforming the mind through daily discipline. How might these principles be applied to your own life?

2. Jean described how she fought these negative attitudes by building regular habits into her walk with God.
   - What were they?
   - Have you developed similar disciplines? What would be good habits for you to cultivate?

3. Each write down or share together in prayer five reasons for thanking God today.

On the sidelines

Glenn Myers

In 1997, aged 35, I almost died. Never since have I been so grateful for the word 'almost'.

I lay on my bed, blue, hyperventilating and with my heartbeat somewhere north of 200 beats per minute and rising. I could have gone into cardiac arrest at any time. I was losing consciousness, doomed as a beached fish, until the paramedics rushed into our bedroom and pressed an oxygen mask to my face.

They carried me on a stretcher past my kids, aged five and three, who had helped the ambulance-people find the house, past some anxious-looking neighbours and brought me to a unit in the hospital where I was almost the only patient, and where the doctor never left the room. Over the next several hours my heartbeat fell back to normal.

I wanted to wear the oxygen mask for the rest of my days, but they forced me to give it back when they rolled me to the ward.

So began a theme-park ride through denial, false dawns, fear, some crying in the night all the way to what feels like contentment and a kind of healing – as good a journey as I've ever been on.

It was all going so well

Life in my little world had been going so well. In 1996 I had signed a deal to write a series of books describing church and missions in frontier settings all around the world. This was a dream I had nurtured and worked towards for a long time. Installed as 'writer in residence' for WEC International in the UK I was now looking forward to years of travelling, researching and writing.

I was busy in our local church and was flattered when on occasions the mission's leadership called me in for a chat.

My wife Cordelia and I were happily married but I was dimly aware that we had some unresolved issues. What came first, for example, family or work? And why were we not very good at leading a housegroup together? (Answer: because I always took over.) In my characteristic way I had tried to avoid or jolly my way around these problems. I was running around doing many things, serving the Lord, busy and really quite important. My wife's meek disapproval was – well it was probably OK really.

The events leading up to my almost-death were thus entirely in character and perhaps in one way or another, inevitable. I was planning a research trip to West Africa, so I had my teeth fixed before I left. I felt fluey afterwards and couldn't shake it off. Cordelia wasn't happy for me to be flying to the tropics while clearly unwell. (I was born with heart abnormalities, so I had to be a little extra careful.)

On the other hand, I'd spent a long time setting this trip up. It was important. I couldn't cancel now. The Lord would provide.

On Cordelia's insistence I phoned our local medical practice. A nurse and I agreed it was probably some virus or a cold. So, off I flew. My 'cold' was endocarditis, which is things growing on the lining of the heart. People with heart disease who have their teeth fixed are especially susceptible. It's typically fatal unless treated.

It's almost funny what happened on that trip. The mission building caught fire a few hours after I arrived. I had to sprint, carrying all my bags, to catch the ferry across the Gambia River. That nearly finished me right there. I was waking in the night with cold sweats. I could hardly stand up. I had to curtail parts of my trip, in particular missing a journey through the Sahara to do some interviews in the Senegal River Valley.

I was still ill when I returned home. I again declined my wife's encouragement to see a doctor and a week later, on a pitch-and-putt course with my Dad, ahead by a couple of holes as I recall, my heart started the downward spiral that a few hours later led to the oxygen mask and the ambulance.

Loss

I was in hospital for a month, then off work for two more months. Cordelia cancelled all my commitments and I stayed at home reading *War and Peace*. I thought I had recovered. But this was only the start of a rather difficult period – scrabbling to find a foothold for my new life.

The doctors spent the next year or two considering some drastic replumbing of my heart – a dangerous operation and a difficult decision. I started applying for disabled benefits from the government, hating the thought of the blue badge with its wheelchair symbol. Twice I was woken in the night with chest pains so severe I couldn't lift my head. Those were curious moments, lying next to my sleeping wife, wondering if this was the end, or if the morning would arrive and I'd wonder what the fuss was about.

My month in hospital had coincided with my son's fourth birthday. They'd all gone for a ride on a little train and brought the birthday cake into the ward afterwards. I was rather haunted by the thought that I almost never saw his fourth birthday at all, and by the further thought that the cause of death would not really have been endocarditis but self-importance and not listening to my wife.

I became quite worn down with all this. I remember walking from the car to the house one time, fed up of the worry, the chest pains, the uncertainties about the future, the sense of trying to keep my head above water. I was fed up of being broken. I was even tired of praying about it. 'Jesus,' I remember saying, 'I don't want answers: but can I just hold your hand?'

Eventually the doctors decided not to operate, which took a great burden away. After a treadmill test, I was awarded my disability benefits. The natural processes of loss and realignment worked through my heart. My feet found solid ground.

Healing

I was asked to work on the final stages of a book called *Healing and Wholeness*. The author had often prayed for people to be healed and had seen some miraculous improvements. He himself had lived with chronic illness for many years, never being cured but far outlasting the doctor's expectations. He had reflected biblically on this.

Robert Hillman's book taught me that 'healing' in the Christian sense is about the whole person, not just the diseased organ. True healing is about the quality and fruitfulness of life. That's why the New Testament (in the book of James, for example) sets healing firmly within a wider context of pastoral care. It's also why issues like lifestyle, diet and relationships are as important as the laying on of hands.

This book made a huge amount of sense to me. I had gone up, and at times been pushed up, to get prayer for healing at all kinds of Christian events. Unfortunately I have never been able to believe God for an instantaneous replumbing of my great arteries and it had never happened.

I could believe God, however – and I came to believe him – for years of full, quiet, productive life and that when my time comes to leave this planet, it will be with a sense of a life fulfilled, not a life cut short. This confidence didn't come all at once, nor did it come quickly, nor did it come through concentrating hard, but it did come. It addressed my deepest fears, it was a gift, and I still live in the good of it.

On The Sidelines

Priorities

I read a second book: *The Complete Idiot's Guide to Managing Your Time*. I'd bought this book before my illness, hoping to find advice on how to squeeze more things into my day. I read it after my illness (if memory serves). I did find some time-management tips that were useful but the book's basic approach was far more drastic. Cut down. Do less. Figure out your priorities, stick to these, ignore the rest. This was a revelation.

I spent time thinking about priorities and making lists (I still do). What was important, really?

To my surprise, succeeding at work wasn't high on the list. It had seemed very high once. The fact that my work had elements of Christian vocation about it had pushed it still higher in my mind. Now when I looked at it, fulfilling a calling by neglecting my wife and kids was not fulfilling a calling at all. It was abusing a calling. There had to be a better way.

Second, I realized that I really enjoyed feeling busy and important. Rushing in from one meeting, gobbling down some tea, and rushing out to another had seemed quite fulfilling once. It seems absurd now.

So I made some resolutions, which can be summarized like this:

1. Don't die of foolishness. Live within my physical means. Do everything I can to stay well. Watch my diet. Spend most nights at home. Take a siesta. Enjoy sunsets. Go on plenty of holidays. Go see the doctor when my wife suggests it. Buy a dog.

2. Family versus work. There are too many books in the world and I've written a few of the surplus stock. The world isn't short of writers. But I'm all my family have by way of spouse or dad. I resolved to be around for my children and in the future if there was a conflict between family and job my 'career' could go hang. Never mind if that means some jobs get left undone or even I disappoint people. So be it. The world won't end.

3. Find my vocation. The theologian Frederick Buechner wrote about looking for your vocation 'where your deep gladness and the world's deep hunger meet.' That's a fine ideal, and a great principle, but it does leave a problem in that many jobs need doing but aren't exactly a source of 'deep gladness'. I think we all have to share in doing those. So I resolved (a) to strive to ensure that most of my work-time is spent in the sweet spot of God's calling and (b) to keep evaluating and pruning so all the other stuff – necessary stuff, servant stuff – doesn't capsize the boat.

Conclusion

My illness was eleven years ago.

I am the same weight now as I was then, give or take a few pounds. We eat a healthy diet. Most days I pull on hiking boots and spend an hour in the park or the countryside with the dog, watching the seasons turn. More things have gone wrong with my heart since 1997 but my mobility and quality of life is as good as any time since that year. I don't fear a premature death any more. All that counts as healing for me.

I finished the series of books, but I didn't do a whole lot more travelling. On occasion I saw God provide interviewees in remarkable ways without me leaving home. Later a colleague made trips and held interviews as a researcher on my behalf. Now I'm seeking to develop a whole new series of books that I believe is a further stage of where 'my deep gladness and the world's deep hunger' coincide. Have I been sidelined in other aspects of my career? I certainly hope so.

My kids have grown into teenagers, taller, wiser and even – arguably – better looking than me. I've been there as they grew up. Even if I were to win the Nobel Prize for Literature – and believe me, I'm sitting by the phone – the thing in my life I'd be most proud of is being the dad to these beautiful offspring.

Once I stopped going out in the evenings, Cordelia felt free to take an evening a week to develop the church's youth ministry. Working with teenagers by the houseful has been a great joy to her and also (from the sidelines) to me. A few months ago we celebrated ten years of this ministry with a ten-course meal to which everyone who'd ever been part of the youth group was invited, a wonderful and unforgettable evening. All this may never have happened if I hadn't moved out of the way.

Of course we don't know what the future holds. I look around me and see plenty of people who have been through mountainous trials that make my brief illness and entirely manageable disability look like a foothill. I'm humbled by people who've endured bereavement, depression, bad marriages, divorce, or other great losses that we've been entirely spared. I've no idea how we'd cope in that kind of storm.

I'm also aware that many people don't appear to have the option to pursue their vocations as I've had the privilege of pursuing mine. Though I would say we do have more choice than we realize. Many of us can downsize careers, homes, commitments, really we can. Much of our busyness and stress is self-inflicted and unnecessary: I really believe this. And if there are necessary seasons of busyness and sacrifice and difficulty, isn't it true that they don't last forever? I think it is.

So I'm no expert but I have learnt some things from dipping my feet in what the old hymn writers used to call 'the Jordan'. I'd rehearse them to myself like this:

You're not Superman.
You're not indispensable at work.
You are a child of grace.
Find and enjoy your portion – no more.
Live so that you won't regret it when you die.
Don't aim to make the headlines; find the sidelines.
Jesus is the famous one; not us.

Glenn Myers is a writer with WEC UK and the author of more than a dozen books, including the 'Briefings' series, which has sold around

Life Lessons

80,000 copies. He has also written a novel called Paradise (published summer 2010) – www.glennmyers.info

For discussion

1. 'Do everything I can to stay well. Watch my diet. Spend most nights at home. Take a siesta. Enjoy sunsets. Go on plenty of holidays. Go see the doctor when my wife suggests it. Buy a dog.' Read Psalm 127. What does this say about priorities?

2. What comes first: family or work? If you can, produce Biblical evidence in favour of each side of the argument. (For example: Mark 3:31-34, Luke 9:59-62 and 14:26-27, talk about putting Jesus first, before our families. In contrast Mark 7:9-13 talks about family responsibilities not being usurped by serving God.)

3. Is it right to speak of people having a vocation, a special set of tasks that God has equipped you for and called you to do? To what extent is it selfish to pursue a 'calling', leaving other jobs undone for others to do? (See, for example, Ephesians 2:10; Luke 10:38-42)

I waited a long time for the answer to my prayer

Jenny Davies

Does prayer work? Does faith work?
I've asked these questions many times.

I really like an answer to my prayers especially the very earnest ones that I pray. There was one prayer that took 48 years before I saw the answer.

But to go back a little ... My uncle was an enthusiastic good-time guy and then he became a Christian – he was really switched on to the Lord. He wanted everyone to know – I mean everyone! I loved visiting his home as a child. He could make Bible stories come alive and the kids just loved him. After every meal at uncle's place he'd have a prayer time. Everyone had to pray. It was just like Jesus was there in the room with us. I think this is when I realised the power and privilege of prayer. When I was 11 years old, my uncle took me to a big youth gathering and this was when Jesus came into my life, forgave my sin and I became God's daughter for life. It was a wonderful year.

Prayer to me is my lifeblood. I don't think I could have survived all these years in life and Christian ministry if it hadn't been such a big part of my life. Right from the very earliest in my Christian experience I found that prayer was important and I needed to make time to share with God my needs and burdens. One of my prayers was for my dad. He was a committed churchgoer but not happy that I had become a 'fanatical Christian' and I longed, ached for him to receive Jesus as his Saviour. I remember pleading for him on my knees in my bedroom and looking out of the window and seeing him on the tractor working in his vineyard. But I had to wait.

The very first BIG prayer that the Lord answered for me was the provision of a Christian friend. I had lots of friends but no Christian friend my age. Whenever I talked to any of my former friends about Christian things they were embarrassed. I needed someone I could share my heart with, someone I could pray with. A pen pal wrote and told me all about his group of young friends. He said there was a verse in the Bible that said, 'If two of you on earth agree about anything you ask for, it will be done for you by my Father in heaven' (Matthew 18:19). He said, 'Let's agree and ask the Lord for a Christian friend for you.' So we prayed for about 18 months.

During this time I started nursing training in my home town and a new girl came to share a twin room with me at the hospital. Each night after work, I read my Bible and when the lights were out I got out of bed on my knees to pray (so she wouldn't notice – what a coward!!) She did notice but said nothing. One night she came off duty really depressed. She said, 'I'll never make a nurse!' Without thinking I said, 'The Lord can help you.' She burst into tears and replied, 'The Lord won't help me because I'm running away from Him.' She explained that she had gone nursing to get away from her godly parents who were praying for her. I explained how I had become a Christian and then prayed a simple prayer. I went to sleep but she stayed awake under deep conviction. For a whole week she was miserable, so much so that patients would ask 'What is wrong with that nurse?' One week later she went home and read a booklet about a young man who became a Christian and she suddenly realised what she had to do. She gave her life to Jesus and when she came back to the hospital the change was really obvious. Patients and staff noticed and she couldn't stop herself sharing what God had done for her.

Amazing! Suddenly I realised that the Lord had answered my prayer. He'd given me more than I asked (Ephesians 3:20). He'd given me a Christian friend right there in my room! Helga was so keen and full of love for Jesus and wanted everyone to know. Night after night we prayed together and saw her two brothers, some cousins and others come to faith in Jesus as Lord. All became active in their churches, two became missionaries and Helga (my prayed-for-friend) joined WEC and served in Gambia (West Africa) for 18 years, as deputy Australian leader for eight years and in Jordan for a further eight years.

While on staff at Worldview Centre, Tasmania for 27 years, we spent many hours in prayer with our fellow staff. There were so many answers to prayer. One of the biggest areas was trusting God for money and resources to complete what seemed to us a never-ending building programme, as we tried to cope with college expansion. We believed that if we knew that this was right in line with God's will, the Lord could supply what we needed without making public appeals for money. It certainly made us totally dependent on Him to get His guidance and then to expect his supply. The many stories were amazing. I remember the time we had embarked on an ambitious plan to build 18 new apartments. It was a case of believing that the money for each month's bills would come in on time.

We needed $14,000 by March 1st 1985 to pay the building suppliers. As a college we prayed together the week before that God would meet this need. Some gifts came from within the college family and from people outside who had no idea of our specific need. When the staff met on Friday for their weekly meeting, we summarised what was available and what was still needed. When we looked at all the funds at our disposal the balance still owing was $5,006.20. We prayed together but had to leave it with God. At the conclusion of the meeting, our accountant went to her office and was told that somebody had called in and handed in an envelope during the afternoon. When she opened it there was $5,000! Along with the interest in our account the bill could be paid!

Later that year we had a problem with bricks. We had ordered enough special size bricks for half of the building and when we went back to the manufacturers for the remaining order they said that they had stopped making them. Again we went back to the Lord in prayer and for two years we waited for our Father to change the company's mind. When the bricks finally arrived we were thrilled and at the way that God supplied the $4,000 to pay for them, but then we had another problem – we needed someone to do the brickwork. Amazingly just at that time the Lord sent a man along who needed personal spiritual help and who said that if he could stay for a while he would be pleased to help us in any way. When we asked him what he could do he said, 'I am a bricklayer!' We felt like the returning exiles in Psalm 126:2-3! 'Our mouths were filled with laughter, our tongues with songs of joy … The Lord has done great things for us, and we are filled with joy.'

But it wasn't just a matter of bricks and mortar; lives were more important. I remember praying so often for one student who was just messing around with his life and wasting the gifts that God had given him. Graduation day came and I dreaded hearing a fake testimony. What a shock I got. He stood up and confessed his laxness, asked forgiveness from his fellow-students and the staff – publicly. God had dealt with him the week before Graduation. I just wept with gratitude and praise to our faithful Father God. He and his wife have spent many years since in fruitful ministry in northern Australia.

On another occasion, one of our men students was greatly troubled by a congenital kidney disease. He returned from a regular visit to the doctor one day with the news that he could never go overseas as a Christian worker. He and his wife had been called into Christian service for this very reason and could not accept the doctor's diagnosis. He asked the staff to anoint him with oil and pray for him according to the passage in James 5:13-18. So that's what we did before the whole college community. There were simple believing prayers and anointing in the name of the Lord. Some weeks later after returning from the next visit to the doctor he was smiling all over his face. After tests they could not find any problem with his kidneys. He had been miraculously healed. The proof was seen as he and his wife worked for many years among the Kurds in the Middle East.

Both of our children were dramatically healed in answer to prayer. Jonathan from hepatitis he picked up in Africa and Andrea when she was just nine months old. On this occasion, Andrea had been choking from an upper respiratory infection. We only just got her to the doctor in time. After ten days in hospital she was still having high fevers and the doctors did not know what else to do. Back home with us, one night she woke up very sick with a high temperature and on the verge of a fit. We were so worried. We sponged and changed her and gave her some fluids. Then suddenly we realised that we should pray for her. Evan and I anointed her and prayed desperately for the Lord to touch her little body. She settled and went to sleep for the rest of the night. The next morning she was like a new baby with no sign of the fever or the awful cough. She never had it again. The Lord had worked a miracle. We are still in awe of our powerful loving God and worship Him.

The Lord does not always heal in the way we think He should. Sometimes we have prayed and anointed someone with oil but not seen a direct healing. Many people around the world prayed earnestly for my sister-in-law Miriam, but the Lord did not give physical healing. He took her home to Himself in the middle of her missionary career. It's His business to heal or not as He thinks fit. Our job is to ask and trust.

All this time I was still praying for my dad. He had had serious farming accidents and major crises in his life, yet in spite of the letters I wrote urging him to hand his life over to Jesus and the prayers I prayed, nothing happened. Dad and mum came to visit us at Worldview many times during our 27 years on staff. He didn't say much but I could tell he was impressed by the College lifestyle. Everyone worked hard, the farm and garden produced well, the property was in excellent condition and the staff and students with their children were a happy bunch, including his two grandchildren. Dad was a hardworking farmer and he often said, 'If you don't work you shouldn't eat' (2 Thess 3:10)!

During the twelve years we spent as Deputies and then International Directors of WEC based in England, prayer was a major part of our lives. It needed to be as we had many huge challenges that had to be resolved. One was the need to trust God for our overseas travel expenses. We visited fields and sending bases for three to five months every year. Some of them contributed generously to our expenses but there were those who were unable to do so. We made it a policy to accept invitations to visit without any financial commitment on their side. Sometimes we had to pay two or even three trips ahead.

I remember one month when our bank account was zero and we still had to pay £400 to the travel agent. Nobody knew about our specific need. We had been praying and trusting for weeks and nothing had happened. Now on the last day payment was due. That morning in our joint prayer time we were pleading with the Lord for his provision. I was in tears and could not understand why the Lord had not answered our prayers. When we had finished our time with the Lord, Evan went off to the office and with a very heavy heart I began to tidy our unit. Shortly after Evan returned with a big smile and said, 'Guess what? The Lord has answered our prayers!' One of our friends from Unimatco (a supply agency associated with WEC which supplied many missions around the world) had stopped him as he came downstairs and said, 'We'd like to give you our tithe this month; we have put £400 in your account.' What a tremendous relief, what joy! I felt rebuked for my lack of faith. The eleventh hour answers are always scary for me!!

Every morning Monday to Thursday in the International Office we met for prayer at coffee time with our colleagues and on Friday we had an extended time sharing in praise and intercessory prayer for the teams around the WEC world. We saw some marvellous answers to prayer (some we are still expecting to see). I remember vividly the agony we felt over two of the teams overseas. We spent hours pleading with the Lord regularly for these teams. Various ones in the International Office visited them to help and negotiate. We saw attitudes change for the better, forgiveness given and received, new staff brought in to help and carry the load. In one situation things changed within two years, the other one is just happening as I write. In answer to believing prayer we have seen visas granted that looked impossible, new work started in tough countries, a new training school started in Canada, leadership seminars developed on a regular basis, the Latino work take off in a new and exciting way and many other answers.

We have seen prayer taking place in interesting ways. A group of four of us went to a restricted country for two weeks specifically to pray for a breakthrough. We spent three to six hours a day in prayer, sometimes with the local workers as well as prayer-walking round town. We are still waiting to see the Lord break through in a big way in that area. Four or five mornings a week Evan and I would go walking (to keep fit) and at the same time praying for the burdens on our hearts and the various needs written on cards in our pockets. Evan often received terrific thoughts or ideas while we were in prayer together.

Then 48 years after I started praying for my dad, I went home for my dear mother's funeral. Her death came suddenly and dad was so distressed. He only wanted to die. I said to him, 'But you can't die that easily.' 'But I want to,' he replied. So I took the plunge and said to him, 'Dad, aren't you afraid to die?' He looked at me and with a big smile and said, 'No, I'm ready to meet the Lord.' What joy filled my heart! Suddenly I realised that my long-time prayers were answered. Afterwards I was able to pray with him daily and when the doctor told him that he had a very aggressive form of leukaemia he smiled and said, 'The Lord has answered my prayer.' Five days later he passed away peacefully only three weeks after my mother had died. I was able to testify at his funeral that the Lord Jesus answers prayer even if it takes 48 years.

What a great God we serve! What a privilege and delight coming to him in prayer every day! My husband Evan and I pray together almost every day. This has been a wonderful bonding experience in our marriage and we have seen and still see so many answers to prayer. Now that we are 'retired' we keep praying and in fact have more time than ever before. We travel regularly quite a distance to see our children and four beautiful grandchildren and to attend the local WEC prayer meeting. We use this time to read and pray through any long letters we receive from WEC workers all over the world. One drives, the other reads and both pray! That has become a very quick journey and over the months we are seeing results. We usually have a lovely calendar on our toilet door giving overseas prayer points (this year Kazakhstan!). What a great opportunity to spend many minutes over the year praying for these fantastic countries! We share prayer points with our church friends at our home meeting as well as giving time most mornings to systematically covering world needs.

Many times the Lord has answered our faith and prayers and what a 'WOW!' experience that is! They have left an indelible impression on my life. I have seen how our heavenly Father answers prayer whether instantly or over many months or years. He is able and does answer the believing, persistent prayers of his children and one day in heaven we will see the full panorama.

Jenny Davies was born and trained as a nurse in South Australia before she went to WEC's Missionary Training College in Tasmania as a student and for 27 years as a staff member. Her experience in WEC's International Office brought her into contact with many missionaries on many fields. Jenny and Evan have two children and four grandchildren.

I waited a long time for the answer to my prayer

For discussion

1. Go round the group: what struck you as you read Jenny Davies' chapter?

2. Share some stories of answered prayer in your personal experience.

3. Look at James 5:13-18. How well does that passage describe your own church practice? In what ways ought you to change?

These foolish things
Byung Kook Yoo

What pleasure my wife Boin and I were feeling as we began our second home leave. Our first years in Gambia had been very difficult with unendurable heat, few available staple provisions, and very few responding to the message to follow Jesus.

Now though, we were getting along so much better in the poor living conditions. The heat was still hard to put up with, but it was getting endurable. Actually, as time went by, it was simply that we had learned to endure it. Our human bodies were proving adaptable to the harsh environment. There was also increased availability of foods at the markets, more frequent availability of electricity, and easier access to a constant water supply so daily life was so much easier than when we had begun.

What was really giving us pleasure, though, as we left Gambia for furlough was the joy of seeing our local disciples one by one beginning to go out into their own ministries. There had been so much labor in prayer and time spent training them but now we could enjoy the fruits of those efforts. We were looking forward to returning to such an on-going ministry rather than facing again those difficult first years in the field.

In the midst of these feelings of joy and expectations, we stopped by the WEC International Office in England as we began the furlough, before traveling on to Korea. Dietrich Kuhl, the International Director confided in us, 'One of the Koreans in WEC must return from the field to Korea to set up a Sending Base. Now is the time to do this. Would you think that there would be anybody who wants to go?'

Though we heard the anxiety and eagerness in his question, my wife and I responded only with politeness, being filled with our own joy and expectations of the furlough awaiting us. 'Yes, someone should do it. Perhaps there will be someone,' we answered with no real interest. We walked out of the room with not another thought of what was indeed someone else's business.

Our furlough time was as wonderful as all of the dreams we had conjured up during those final weeks in Africa. We had much time to spend with our children and show them sights around Korea that they barely remembered. Indeed, our youngest had not even been born at our last home leave and we were eager to introduce her to her homeland.

Unexpectedly, in the midst of the furlough, the Deputy International Director of WEC, Evan Davies, informed us that he wanted to come for a visit and spend time with us. What a good idea we thought. We guessed that he recognized the need to learn more about Korea, and that we were to be his tutors!

During his ten-day visit, we took him to the old palaces, famous churches, and beautiful countryside to show him the culture, history, and geography of Korea. Surprising to us, though, Evan did not seem to show much interest during most of the tours.

Still uncertain if we had met his needs or interest during his stay, we drove him to the airport for his return flight and waited for him to complete the check-in. He asked us to accompany him to a corner of the passenger lounge and sit down for a moment. Then, at the last minute, he began to explain to us why he had come to Korea.

'Byoung Kook and Boin, listen to me! Could both of you wrap up your ministries in Africa and come to Korea to set up the Korean Sending Base? A servant of God needs to work where God wants him. It is important work that you are doing in your small country in Africa, but I hope that you will consider the whole of our organization instead of just your small part and that you will take the time to pray about the organization's need. We regard the "pillar of sacrifice" as a core value in WEC. Sometimes we need to lay down our personal plans and ministries and give them up for the need of the organization. The International Office and I will pray for you for the Lord's guidance.'

Evan suddenly turned and walked directly to the departure gate, leaving us unable to respond. Still sitting on the bench, we puzzled over this unexpected request, now realizing the true purpose behind his trip to Korea.

Our thoughts and conversation raced: What was he saying? Did Evan really mean for us to move back to Korea? What was to happen to the ministries in Africa? What would our sending church and denomination say if this change in plan were to happen?

Our thoughts then moved on in confusion to the idea of the Sending Base itself: How do you establish a Sending Base? Has Evan considered or even knew how hard it would be to run a Sending Base in Korea? He made it sound like we should just find a building and open for business, but instinctively Boin and I knew that it must be much more complicated than that.

Our confusion settled on the final issue: Why us? There seemed to be several other Koreans we know in WEC who would be much more capable. Their careers had strengths that would help in this kind of new endeavor.

We continued to sit on the bench where Evan had left us, too confused to get up and go back to our home yet. His words that 'Sometimes we need to lay our personal plans and ministries down and give them up for the need of the whole organization and for the Lord' kept circling in our thoughts, along with his reminder of the 'pillar of sacrifice' that is often referred to by WEC.

Evan had only used a few words by his challenge to us, but I began to feel the pressure of the importance of this decision. It was not just a prayer request. It had the potential of turning our personal world upside down. 'Why on earth did he drop in on our furlough and destroy the good time that we were having?' I asked myself. I wanted to be able to set aside the words he had just spoken to us and return to the peace and enjoyment of the week but I knew that would not be possible.

As we returned home my mind continued to try to wrap some sort of understanding around this very unexpected request. Perhaps Evan had indeed recognized that there were others better qualified than us, but they had turned him down. Then I reasoned, 'Okay, he asked us, but we just need to say "No" also and return to our furlough and go back to Africa.'

Conflicting thoughts began to pop up within my spirit. This new challenge may indeed come from the Lord. This furlough may have been timed to begin to wean us from Africa in order to prepare us to return to Korea. What should I be doing if this was from the Lord? Suddenly, fear and confusion entered my heart. There was not much time left to make this decision before we would be automatically returning to Africa.

During the weeks since Evan's unexpected prayer request it was obvious that Boin and I were each approaching Evan's request differently. Boin had responded with more apparent calm than I had, showing no anxiety over seriously considering the request and actually becoming irritated every time I used the phrase 'going to Korea' in our discussions. She apparently had already prayed and decided that Evan had simply asked a question that did not concern her, as the answer was 'No'. She had been able to return to the enjoyment of the furlough as planned, having a delightful time together with the children.

These Foolish Things

It was I who kept circling in confused thoughts about how to resolve Evan's words to us. My complaint was that we had worked hard to learn to live in Africa with the heat and the deprivations. We had worked hard to begin the ministry. The more I thought about moving away from it, the more I began to agree with Boin's conclusion that the organization's need for a Sending Base did not concern me – it was none of my personal business.

Unlike my wife, however, the conflict would not leave me alone. I could not continue to enjoy the furlough as if the prayer request to come to Korea had not been asked. Many nights my body failed to fall asleep as my thoughts kept churning in my head. There was an ongoing concern about this decision that did not release me. I could not just go on with our plans for Africa without knowing for sure that we were not to return to Korea.

'Maybe we are going against the Lord,' I thought. Finally, I persuaded my wife, my dear life partner and co-worker, to go with me to the Prayer Mountain for a week of praying and fasting to make sure that we were sincerely seeking God's will over this request to start the Sending Base.

Boin has a wonderful contemplative nature and agreed to go gladly. On this occasion, though she agreed to come to partner with me in seeking a final decision, she herself was not experiencing the conflict that I was. Since there was so little time left before we needed to leave for Africa, we agreed to set a limited time – one week. We prayed before we left 'Lord, we can only be at this prayer mountain six days and five nights. Please speak to us as we are going to fast and pray.'

The first few days at the Prayer Mountain were difficult for me. The conflicting thoughts kept running through my mind day and night as I tried to pray. 'Lord, what is this all about? What shall we do? We really want to go back to Gambia. There are many things to do there. You know that we cannot possibly be the best-qualified people of this new task.'

Not only could I not stay focused with my prayers, I had difficulty with the fast. My body was very weak; after two days I needed to change my fast from fasting through all meals, to choosing instead to fast for only one meal a day. I could not hold to even these spiritual disciplines as I tried to seek God's will.

On the other hand, my dear wife, who came only because I requested that we go, continued to fast resolutely trying to obey our decision to seek God through prayer and fasting during this week.

As the week progressed, I continued to look for some sort of dramatic answer from God. As I became weaker, I secretly hoped that maybe Boin, with her intense praying and fasting, would be led to an understanding of what God's answer was for our dilemma, but there was no sign or confirmation.

Finally, it was the last day that we could stay at the mountain – the end of the week that we had set aside for seeking God's will. 'Well that's it then' I concluded. 'We came to ask God, and have found no answer that we are to accept the request for the Sending Base, so we are free to go pack up our things and head back to Africa. We have given God a chance to speak within our spirit.'

The evening meeting was over on our last night's stay. On the way to our room, I noticed a group of believers gathered to pray. My feet moved toward the edge of the group and I sat down among them. Yes, it felt right to join in on this final prayer time, trying to make sure that I had done all the praying I could during this week.

The prayer time followed a simple format. Someone would stand and give a request – a health concern, job need, family issues; the group would then pray for several minutes for that person.

As I listened to the requests, I found myself rationalizing in discouragement why I myself could not go forward. It would be too difficult to explain the complicated decision that we were facing in the brief time before the group. Also, as missionary, I felt separated from the everyday nature of the concerns being raised. Somehow, in my self-centered focus, my prayer request seemed to me to be on a different level. They would not be able to understand my situation or know how to properly pray for it.

I failed to see the presumption on my part that it apparently was also a tough request to ask of God since he had not been able to answer it yet during the week.

Without being aware that I was actually moving, I found that I had stood up as if pushed from behind. God must have gotten tired of my rationalizing and moved me forward to ask for prayer. I gave a brief summary of my prayer request, providing what I considered to be the prayer points: 'I am a missionary who is working in Africa. I came home for furlough and it is now time for us to go back to the field. During this time, we have received a request to wrap up the ministries there and come to Korea to start an inland mission. To tell the truth, my ministries in Africa are so important that I believe that I should go back there and continue working. I don't have any idea what to decide about this new request so I am praying. Please pray with me.'

As I stood there feeling awkward, I knew that I was also hoping to convey to them the real thoughts behind my request. I wanted them to agree with my true feelings, that all of them should think that it is right for me to go back and continue the work. This was really the answer that I was seeking.

The kind group began to pray for my request just like they had for the others, praying out loud over the next five minutes when they felt led. As I sat in their midst, I sensed someone moving nearby and instinctively opened my eyes. In front of me, a note had been placed on my Bible. On it was written 'Dear Missionary. God wants you to work in Korea. The Holy Spirit spoke this to me clearly.' I picked up the note and looked quickly around, but couldn't tell who had laid the note.

Grinning, I put the note into my Bible. I was so startled at the answer that I actually sniggered to myself in embarrassment. 'Dear me, Lord! Why didn't you tell me this answer directly instead of through others? Is my spirit not on the level of another that I could not hear Your answer? You want to give the task for Korea to a poorly prepared person like me? Oh, Lord!' I left the prayer group and finished the journey back to our room. Finally, during the final hours of the prayer week, I was able to sleep soundly.

The story, however, did not end in victory. Though I had prayed for an answer, and received an answer, I did not accept the answer. I didn't even tell my wife that I had received an answer in a note written by someone else!

Instead, I found myself angered that some thoughtless person had the audacity to presume to leave for me such an important message as if it was an answer from God. This was a message that would determine the future of a missionary, and they hadn't even signed his or her name. Was he or she also going to take any responsibility for the results of that answer?

Though I was denying that the note contained an answer to the decision of what we were to do, I did not have peace as we came down from the Prayer Mountain. 'If this was really from God, and the voice of the Holy Spirit, then I am directly disobeying the Holy Spirit,' I told myself. The last days in Korea flew past as I continued to be filled with mixed feelings about understanding what God's answer was to the request for our starting the Sending Base.

We went back to our field in Africa without informing our friends there that there had been any other plan. But God was good to us. Even in our confusion, we did believe that God was our leader, and that when He says 'Come', we come; and when He says 'Go', we go. Though we had not been able to discern His voice while we were on furlough, and though I ignored the note that was in my Bible, after we returned to Gambia and began to work in our ministries again, God presented to our hearts a clear calling. We wrapped up our ministries in Africa and came back to Korea to set up a Sending Base.

Looking back on our time at Prayer Mountain, the person who gave me the note appeared to have heard the voice of God right, while I turned out to be a hopeless missionary that could not rely on others to decide on a life matter, just as Eli could not. For sure, it was not because of the note that we received enough courage and faith to leave Africa. It was the definite clear calling of God that changed our heart. However, that person who passed the message to me must have been a man or woman like Samuel who could rightly catch the voice of the Holy Spirit. I hope that the anonymous believer is one of you reading this story. But there is also one final change: I now accept that God speaks through others to us.

When we returned to Korea, we were overwhelmed with our ignorance: What on earth should we do? Where do we start? Korea was now our new mission field, and we found it almost as hard to begin there as we had found it to begin in the unknown mission field in Gambia 14 years before. We had little understanding of the changes that had happened in the business or church cultures during our absence.

More critical than that, we did not have any knowledge about what was needed to create a functioning Sending Base. This Base was to send missionaries out all over the world. We knew that there had to be a broad range of administrative decisions established to develop the effectiveness of this new mission task.

Boin and I started at the simplest level of establishing the Base; we obtained a room to sit in! A friend loaned us an empty classroom at a learning center. We set it up as our office, putting a sign out front stating 'WEC Korean Sending Base'. We laughed together at the incredulity between the sign's grand idea, and the barren room with no decorations visible through the door. Every morning without fail we went to 'work' and sat in the empty room. What were we to do now?

When we had come back to Korea to begin the Sending Base, we had first dropped in again to the International Office in England. The International Director Dietrich Kuhl had handed us several business cards from Korean pastors whom he had met. These pastors had each visited the WEC International Office and had personally met Dietrich. He had kept these cards very carefully, considering that these pastors may be part of God's plan for helping to establish the Sending Base.

Now that we were 'established' in our office, we used the phone that the learning center had kindly installed and began to follow up these contacts. Some of the name cards had information added to them in ink, either written by the Pastor himself or information provided by Dietrich. The cards had the contact addresses with home phone numbers and mobile numbers of these famous pastors who had asked the WEC International Director to please visit them and their churches when he was in Korea.

Apparently, this courtesy did not extend to ourselves, who were in Korea instead. I made phone calls to some of them, introducing myself as part of WEC, and then extending greetings from Dietrich Kuhl. Their responses were not as expected. Not only were there not any spontaneous offers of cooperation, the individual pastors were not even willing to set up an appointment to discuss any of our hopes or needs. Boin and I started to feel even more hopeless with our daunting task.

There was one final call that I was willing to make. It was actually to the most famous pastor of all who had visited Dietrich. This pastor already knew a great deal about WEC. We considered that his response would most likely be different than the others, as we knew he talked about WEC frequently. I put my hopes, human though they were, all on him being our 'ticket' to getting established. We were able to make an appointment with him, and waited with increasing flutters of hope for that day to arrive.

In my anxiousness to have a good meeting, I arrived one hour early so as not to cause any delays for this very busy man. I confirmed the appointment with the secretary who told me that he could only spare 20 minutes for the interview due to his tight schedule. It was very obvious that he was indeed quite a busy man. There were other people before me and behind me standing in a queue to have word with him. While I waited for the appointed time to arrive, I revised what needed to be said within the short meeting, thinking that perhaps the pastor did not need to hear about WEC again as he was already quite familiar with the mission efforts, but focusing the information instead on our reason for leaving Africa, the reason for

WEC's choice to establish a Sending Base in Korea, and our goals to push forward into the future.

At long last it was my turn. I entered his office with a tense look as if I had a job interview with the President of a company. Being so aware of the short time I had, I poured out at top speed all that I was trying to communicate. The pastor listened to me quietly, then made his own point clearly, but with a gentle smile. 'Your passion is okay, and I know WEC very well. But I want to mention just one thing here. It is too late! It is too late for WEC to come into Korea and start the ministries of recruiting and training missionaries with a Sending Base.

'All of the other international organizations arrived in Korea a long time ago and have already gained their ground in finding those willing to be missionaries. What is more, every Korean denomination and national Korean mission organization is also already doing a good job. In fact, there is a new feeling growing that there is no longer any merit in the international organizations being here as our national groups are doing well on their own.

'Given this present trend, it seems to not be wise for WEC to decide to come to work in Korea at this late date. People won't feel the need for what WEC has to offer, nor will other organizations want to receive any help from you. Personally, I am engaged already with so many things that I myself cannot afford to help you out either. I am sorry.'

There was no reason for me to stay any longer in his presence. My 20-minute interview was over. There was no room for misunderstanding what he was trying to tell me. He had clearly communicated it very succinctly. Walking out of his room, I felt a heavy weight descend on my mind and then bear down on my body. This must be what it feels like to receive a failure notice after a job interview.

My thoughts thudded heavily within me: Would it ever be possible to establish the Sending Base without any help from such a famous pastor? The other mission organizations in Korea had already seen the need for operating on a relational basis with at least several big churches in order to be strong in what they were doing. Who will recognize WEC and give it the same recognition and support that the other mission organizations already had? Certainly this wonderful, famous pastor had given me wise counsel and was not trying to talk nonsense to me.

It may be too late, as the pastor said. Was it really God's will for us to come to Korea? What should Boin and I do now? Wouldn't it be wiser not to invest energy in a plan that was doomed to failure? Actually, I began to complain to myself that it must be the WEC leaders who don't really know the situation in Korea and therefore it is their fault to have set me up in a foolish position? Here Boin and I are, fearlessly following in step with WEC International to come to Korea. We must appear to be just as far behind personally after our years in Africa as the whole WEC group appears to be in its timing.

I continued to pour out my complaints even though I had no one to hear them. I walked down the steps from the pastor's office with heavy feet, feeling alone in the world. It was pitiful that I, who was not good with words and spoke in an inelegant way, had thought that I could make a strong impression on others. What man will come and join an unfamiliar Western organization with my dull challenge? How on earth had I considered that I could set out to win people and churches in Korea over to our mission when here I had failed to even persuade a pastor? It really didn't matter any more anyway. It was obvious that we were too late and our decision to come to Korea must be wrong!

At that moment Boin's face came to my mind. She hated leaving Africa and coming back to Korea; no arguments for our coming back had made sense to her, but she eventually, with tears, agreed to leave Africa, 'I am coming with you just because I can't divorce you,' she had declared honestly, if not kindly. I tried to protect both of us from her attitude, saying ever so solemnly and sincerely that I was asking as a servant of God and not as her husband. 'Honey,' I pleaded, 'if by any chance we face hard times in Korea, please don't ever say, "See!! I told you we should not come to Korea. I knew this would happen". Don't ever say that, okay?'

I was reminded of those words right now. But this time I was saying the words to myself. I was blaming our leadership for sending me out to Korea, and even though I knew that God guides our each and every step, I now doubted even His calling.

Too distressed to continue, I turned my feet back to the church. I wasn't even searching for a place to pray, but needed to sit. There seemed to be no strength in my legs but sitting on the stairs would make me look like a beggar, so I looked for a room with chairs. A spacious meeting room on the first floor caught my sight. As I glanced in I realized that in the corner there were a couple of believers with their heads bowed down as if they were praying.

After plonking myself down in a chair, I closed my eyes but not to pray at all as my attitude in the last few minutes had been against God, not in seeking him in prayer. Instead, I began to argue within myself. 'Where is the knowledge of the times of guidance that you have experienced so far? What are you going to do now in Korea? Why are you focusing on such a grand idea that it makes you feel like you are going to have a big business? Why are you fussing with such tension, trying to get support from these big pastors? You want someone with fame to recognize you? You want their financial support?'

I was actually muttering these arguments as if I had an audience in front of me. Being disappointed in myself, I felt ashamed and new words came to my mind, so different from the previous complaints it was as if God was rebuking me. 'Get this right,' I said to myself. 'Let's not dream to carry on a large business. Let's go about this calling just as I am and as far as I can. In the end there is nothing to lose.' In my spirit, I was encouraged to pick up and begin again, but this time the plan that came to mind was to follow up with other connections that had begun after returning to Korea. These new connections were not very famous men, but serious and unsophisticated ones, following simpler ways.

Life Lessons

Ten years have now passed since I needed to sit down and rest after that disappointing meeting. Starting with the new idea that came that day, the WEC Korean Sending Base became established. In contrast to what had been predicted – that there was no room for WEC in Korea – we have grown in those ten years to a large family of several hundred members made up of candidates, missionaries, staff, and board members. Everywhere we go to speak, we talk with vigor about being a 'faith mission' that is relying on God only, not on the power and prestige of people.

When I look back, I don't think that the Pastor's judgment was wrong that day nor do I think that he was unsympathetic in turning us down. On the contrary, he made me see that I was helpless to do this new ministry. Though it was a difficult encounter with him, if I ever meet him again I will choose not to point out that his prediction was wrong, nor to brag about all the fruit he did not predict, but rather I will show my appreciation to him for helping me understand that we could only proceed by relying on the God who sent us here.

It is now possible to see God's plan in choosing us for this new task. It was God's complete plan to make us into the leaders He needed to run the Sending Base. The fruit that God has developed from this Sending Base is not because of the expertise that we brought with us, for we had none, but because of whom He is. If we had been better suited to begin this job, we then could feel that the fruit came because of what we had learned during our 10 years of experience in Africa, or because of the knowledge we gained working with foreigners in our international organization. But what we know instead is that we cannot do God's mission with our human strength or wisdom. 'Brothers, think of what you were when you were called ... But God chose the foolish things of the world to shame the wise; God chose the weak things of the world to shame the strong.' (I Cor. 1:26-27). That is why God alone is to be glorified and His name is to be lifted high!

Glory be to God, the Almighty One!

These Foolish Things

Byung Kook Yoo is a graduate of Chong-shin University and Hop-dong Theological Seminary. With his wife Boin, he has served as a missionary to the Gambia (West Africa), was the founding director of WEC's Korean Sending Base and is now WEC's International Director of Mission Mobilisation. Byung Kook and Boin have three grown-up children.

You can read about Byung Kook and Boin's African adventures in *The Untold Stories of Missionary Yoo* (2010).

For discussion

1. Byung Kook Yoo uses the quote 'God chose the foolish things of the world to shame the wise; God chose the weak things of the world to shame the strong' (1 Cor. 1:27).

   How does his story demonstrate this? Think of other examples in scripture. Is this a spiritual principle? Have you seen this principle operating in your own or your church's life?

2. Two elements in Byung Kook's calling and preparation for Korea were (a) Receiving nothing after six days of prayer and fasting except a scribbled note from a stranger and (b) A wise and experienced pastor giving him good reasons not to do what he was doing. Why do you think God acted that way in Byung Kook's life? What does that teach us about the way God speaks?

3. Boin Yoo said to her husband, 'I'm only coming back to Korea you because I can't divorce you!' What do you think of her attitude?

Strength out of weakness
(2 Cor 12:9,10)

Dr Helen Roseveare

2008

If I was only to look at the physical events of this year, I might be tempted to call it my 'Annus horribilis'. For nearly fifteen weeks at the start of the year, I knew PAIN .. ever-increasing pain, pain that was untouched by pain-killers, pain that persisted day and night, pain that spread from one shoulder to the other, down the arms, across the chest, eventually down to the thighs ... pain that seemed to dominate my thinking, pain that I could not escape from. Then with it, ever-increasing weakness, weakness that became so marked that I could do very little for myself – becoming dependent on someone else to turn me over in bed, to help me up or to dress.

During this period, fear began to creep in – not fear of dying, nor of death itself, but just that I could not cope. I was so conscious that I could not say with Paul (Phil.4:11,12) 'I have learned to be content whatever the circumstances ... I have learned the secret of being content in any and every situation ...' I was definitely not content with my situation. Yet I knew so well that God had said to

75

me on many occasions: 'My grace is sufficient for you' – therefore sufficient to make me able to be content – but I simply did not know how to take hold on that sufficient grace.

Then a consultant gave the diagnosis: started me on treatment: and in less than 24 hours the pain had gone.

It was almost unbelievable – yet instead of being overwhelmingly thankful for the relief, I was suddenly fearful. Had I learned the lesson that God was graciously and patiently seeking to teach me? Or had I avoided it by almost demanding healing? I knew Psalm 106, verse 15 'He gave them their request but sent leanness into their soul.' (AV) I dreaded that, even more than the pain and weakness.

Then after three months of normal health and activities, I was suddenly smitten by another bug that laid me low with a chest infection for the best part of a month. At the height of the infection, I thought (wrongly) that I was going to die. Once again, fear gripped my heart. Not the thought of dying – and the wonderful joy of going to be with my Saviour, and seeing Him face to face, and being able to worship Him in a manner worthy of Him – no, but I was stupidly conscious of not having my affairs in order, so as to make it easy for anyone should I die. I knew I needed to re-write my will, and in the midst of a severe infection and toxic muddle-headedness, this matter seemed so important!

What was God trying to teach me, through all this? Once more, I was utterly dependent on others to care for me, to hold me and encourage me in the moments of spasm, and inability to get a breath … was I listening to what God was saying to me?

Can we go back to the beginning of this particular lesson?

I have been a STRONG character all my life – at least, that is what others have always thought! The second of five children, I held my own in family disputes. My mum probably found me headstrong: my siblings merely said, 'pig-headed!' – possibly, strong-willed would have been a kinder assessment. At school, I always had to be the top of class in every subject – not because of any deliberate desire to beat other girls, but essentially to beat myself – and to please my father.

Strength out of Weakness

But under the apparent strong exterior, there was a weakness – unrealised by myself at the time. I nursed an inferiority complex, a need to be loved and appreciated. Going off to boarding school as a twelve-year-old, I probably fantasised that I wasn't loved by my parents, and I began to create my own world, without much reference to truth and accuracy. Yet through seven years (including most of the years of World War II) a hunger began to grow in my heart for … I'm not sure for what exactly … or for Whom … but for a 'power' to control me, guide my life, and above all to love me.

Starting at University, knowing no-one, lonely and not a little frightened, yet terrified of disappointing my parents, I found myself unsatisfied with the religious practices in my life up to that time – church every Sunday: regular attendance at Sunday School: confirmed as a fourteen-year-old – but with no knowledge of the Saviour and His love. I began to search elsewhere for an answer to the deep questions. What was life all about? Was there a purpose to it all? Where did I fit in? I went to meetings of the Communist Party, and listened to talks on Dialectical Materialism. I went to meetings of the Christian Science Group, and heard talks on Mind over Matter. Fortunately for me, by God's grace, the Christian Union girls then invited me to join them at some of their meetings – and at last, something seemed to make sense. The Lord drew me to Himself, and the sheer explosive wonder of coming to know the Saviour, and that He knew me and loved me, and had died to save me, completely turned my life upside down!

The joy of telling others about the Lord Jesus, and what He had done for us in dying for us on the Cross, took possession of me. Sunday School teaching, Christian Union meetings, Bible Study, prayer and missionary meetings filled every gap in my medical-study programme. Going to the Keswick Convention, and having my sense of call to missionary service confirmed – that wonderful old hymn: 'Stir me, O stir me, Lord, I care not how, but stir my heart in passion for the world' – set the direction for my life from then on.

Yet, within less than a year, a nagging doubt started. Was this sense of call just 'STRONG me' wanting to serve the Lord, or was it really a call from God?

I finished at University with a degree in medicine and went to the WEC Missionary Centre to be trained for work overseas, needing to learn to submit to authority without questioning everything, and how to work in a team and not just as an individual. Again, my strong personality appeared to several members of Mission Leadership as a handicap. Maybe this had been commented on to the Leadership out in Congo, for when I was eventually accepted into membership, and had packed and sailed for Africa and arrived at the village of Ibambi in the great rain-forest of central Africa, it was as though I had been pre-judged – as though my fellow missionaries expected me to be cock-sure, even arrogant, and self-sufficient. In fact, I was fearfully lacking in self-confidence, and deeply conscious of my inadequacy to be the doctor they had all prayed for, and who was expected to be able to do everything, from paediatrics to geriatrics, medical and surgical. I needed support and encouragement … but God knew that I needed to trust Him for that, and not just fellow missionaries.

With my team of African helpers, we needed to build a hospital. This included making bricks, burning bricks, putting bricks on bricks – and my knowledge of such affairs was nil. Learning together from an English textbook, and with the help of a local Belgian coffee-planter, we threw ourselves into the task – and immediately I was known to be strong, and determined, and capable of leading the work forward. Years later, my closest Congolese girl-friend, Mama Taadi, asked by a visitor how she remembered me from those early days, her one-word answer was 'Strong!'

Yet as I look back, my own consciousness of those days was my weakness – my fear of being a failure – and the many times of physical sickness when I could not cope alone. Was God already speaking to me back in those early days? Were my drive and my independent spirit getting in the way of the work that He, the Lord God Almighty, wanted to do in and through my African colleagues and myself?

Strength out of Weakness

On one occasion, I was found by my colleague, John Mangadima, on the floor of my home, unconscious, at 2pm. It was a Tuesday afternoon when I should have been in college, lecturing nurses. John made the diagnosis, started the treatment, and organised all the care I needed. When I began to recover on the Thursday afternoon, I had to say, 'Thank you!' to John and the team of nurses for all they had done for me – instead of them saying 'Thank you!' to me – which was the usual way round. Was God saying to me, yet again, 'Allow yourself to be vulnerable, to be known to be needy: don't always be self-sufficient and able to cope; allow your colleagues to feel that they are needed too!'?

But was I listening? I just felt that I was a nuisance to the team when I was ill. Someone, who already had a full load of their own, had to look after me: another had to add my load to theirs, until I recovered.

During my first furlough, I made up my mind that I would not go back unless I was married. It wasn't really the loneliness; I never minded being alone. No, it was carrying the final responsibility for making important decisions. I didn't mind hard work; I was willing to attempt things that I had never done before – be it building a hospital, or doing an emergency operation – but the deciding as to when such should be done, I shrank from this. I wanted to pass the buck to someone more capable, better trained. But God was saying over and over again, 'Trust Me! You can always pass the buck to Me and I will carry it for you!' Again, was I listening? Or did I not really believe God, nor believe in His ability to carry the buck for me?

Going back to Congo in 1960, at the time when the country became independent from the Belgians, I faced new and even more overwhelming situations. Most of the Belgian doctors in our north-eastern Province had left when the Congolese army mutinied after the Declaration of Independence. I was suddenly called on to handle medical emergencies far beyond my competence, and there was no-one else to turn to for help or advice. I had stayed on at Nebobongo when most other Europeans had evacuated, because I was sure that God had brought me back to the country for 'such a time as this'. But even that assurance was insufficient to keep me at peace when troubles erupted all around us. We were threatened by marauding bands of undisciplined soldiers. We were shouted at by local village elders, who felt we should have handed over leadership of the hospital (and doubtless of its accounts) to a Congolese man. Desperately sick and injured folk were brought in by stretcher from near and far, as there was nowhere else to take them ... and I was the only doctor still functioning in the area.

The team at our hospital leant on me for everything – was I not strong enough to carry them all? Little did they know how fear dogged my actions every day, and every night. But I sensed that I must not show my inner weakness; for their sakes I must at least appear strong.

I remember very clearly another situation that developed over the amount we paid our workforce. There was a Government minimum wage, but we made all our nurses and workmen sign a voluntary declaration that they agreed to accept what we could afford, even though that was considerably less than the minimum. In my mind, I was aware that to make them sign such an agreement may well have contradicted the sense of the word 'voluntary' – but humanly speaking, it was totally unrealistic to think of paying more than we did. John Mangadima had by then been elected Chief of Administration for our medical services, even though I was still known as the Medical Superintendent. Doubtless urged on by discontented workmen, John put forward a case, demanding higher wages for everyone employed by our Medical Services. This was transferred to higher authority, and the day came when we were visited by the local Chief of Zone. He called a meeting of myself (with two supporters) and John Mangadima (and his two supporters). I had fear in my heart. If the case was cut against me, and possibly backdated to the Day of Independence, I could be fined hundreds of pounds – or be imprisoned for years! The argument went to and fro and then Authority demanded to see one of their pay-books. He read the statement that they had each signed voluntarily. He then turned on John and his two helpers, and said: 'You are fools! By being employed by the missionaries you have everything lined up for eternity: by choosing to join those of us employed by the State, you might enjoy some things in the now, but have nothing for eternity!' I could hardly believe my ears! I glanced at my two faithful supporters – Mama Taadi and Mama Damaris – and they could barely hide their delight! We thanked Authority, and I went to prepare them coffee – and broke down and cried. The relief was so overwhelming.

Did I not then realise that my weakness and fear had been completely overridden by God's strength and provision? Could I not learn the lesson that He was repeatedly and patiently teaching me?

Then we were caught up in the civil war of the mid-'sixties. Rebel soldiers flooded the area and threatened us all with indescribable consequences if we did not do exactly what they wanted when they wanted it. They had guns and we did not. Once again, fear became a silent stalking force, day and night. We could almost taste fear when these evil men came into the village, even before we saw or heard them. They demanded food ... and money ... and our watches ... and anything else that caught their fancy. They accompanied me on ward-rounds in the hospital, and told me which patients I should select for surgery. If I argued, I would be struck across the face with the butt end of a gun. I didn't argue. Many local people were savagely beaten up.

Then the night came when a group of these evil men broke into my home around midnight, smashing china, throwing books out of their shelves on to the ground, searching for any hidden treasure. Angered when they found nothing, they turned on me. I sought to flee, but they found me: dragged me to my feet, struck me, breaking my glasses: flung me down again and cruelly kicked me, breaking my back teeth. They threatened to kill me, and I almost wished they would and finish off the cruel charade.

Where was God? Had He left me to suffer at the hands of these unpredictable guerrilla soldiers? Why couldn't God protect me? I had given all to serve Him there in the Congo. I felt so intensely weak … 'God, where are You?' my heart cried. Driven down the corridor of my home at the point of a gun, God Himself spoke into my tortured heart. 'Can you thank Me …' – no way! – half-a-minute, listen: 'Can you thank Me for trusting you?'

That was an amazing thought! I always thought of me trusting God, but never of Him trusting me. In other words, yes, He could have rescued me out of the situation; He could have prevented the situation ever arising; but He was trusting me in it, somehow as part of His wonderful over-all purpose. 'Can you thank Me for trusting you with this situation, even if I never tell you why?'

Even in the midst of the terror of that night, I managed to whisper to God, 'Yes, thank You. If You have some purpose in all this, even though I cannot see it or understand it now, thank You for trusting me to be part of Your programme!' and even in the midst of pain and fear, an enormous peace enveloped me. Indeed, God's strength had replaced my weakness – but I didn't see it like that at the time.

Dragged away, thrown up in a truck and driven off to an unknown destination through the darkness of that night, fear again raged in my heart. Yet, fighting with the fear, was this newly received sense of the peace of God's intervention. I was horribly conscious of my own weakness, and barely realised God's strength to keep me through it all. Yet looking back later, hindsight taught me some big lessons from that night, but they were lessons I was going to have to learn over and over again. I seemed unable, or at least unwilling, to take in the lesson, and to thank God for His strength as He patiently sought to replace my own weakness with His presence.

Others in our group of missionaries, held together under house-arrest for the next five weeks, seeing how I apparently coped with the suffering, and considering me as *strong*, totally unable to help me in my own frustrating sense of weakness and fear. Years later, when I was invited to take part in one of our Mission's Leaders' Conferences, as a representative of the hundreds of single women missionaries serving all over the world, many of those same singles objected that I did not really represent them because I was strong, and most of them felt very vulnerable and weak. I can remember now how hurt I felt by their lack of understanding, yet was it my own fault that they felt as they did? Did I give an appearance of being able to cope – even of self-sufficiency and strength – when in fact I was wholly conscious of weakness and inadequacy?

Years later – after our rescue from this rebel captivity, a year at home recovering from all the trauma, and after travelling back to Congo to take part in the re-construction and opening of a new medical Centre in the east of the country – I found myself as Director of a new training college for para-medical national workers. Once more there were moments when I doubted if I could cope with seeming impossibilities. Thousands of dollars were needed for the construction of the new college buildings. Every month, as payday for the workmen approached, I feared that there would not be enough available cash to pay them all … yet never once was I unable to pay each one what was needful. Students had to be fed and clothed as well as being taught; finance was needed week by week for supplementary food, besides what we were able to grow; and every week the finance became available.

With the arrival of small battery-powered radios into our area, students began hearing news of the great outer world – of how students in other lands were rebelling against authority and workmen were going on strike for higher wages – and even though they barely understood what was being spoken about, they began to flex their muscles and attempt similar exploits, and I feared that I would not be able to control the explosive atmosphere. That is what eventually occurred in my last few months in the country. The student body rose against me and accused me to the Government of … I'm not exactly sure of what, but basically of misusing college funds. There were no such funds; all the money that went into building the college and into teaching the students all came from personal friends in the homelands who gave sacrificially to support us. But it was a pitting of their strength against my weakness – and

God appeared to allow them to succeed – doubtless to teach me again the same lesson: 'Allow Me to replace your weakness with My strength'. Again, was I really listening?

I came home to the UK to help care for Mother in her increasing frailty, and to share in the home-end ministry of WEC as a deputation speaker all over the English and French-speaking world. Some amazing and often wonderful experiences ensued. God was, as ever, exceedingly gracious and patient. WEC had given me the sense of belonging to a large and caring family for so many years and I wanted to give back all I could in serving them – in whatever direction they chose. Yet deputation ministry was certainly not what I would have chosen! It could involve sleeping in a different bed every day for weeks on end; travelling enormous distances to meet with new people daily; having to adapt quickly to each new situation at a moment's notice, and giving a suitable challenging message for whatever age-group. The work became extraordinarily tiring, as well as being basically very lonely. Living out of a suitcase for months on end, seeking to relate and to be available to any one in any sort of need, writing thousands of letters … No! Not what I would have chosen. I am a home-bird; I dislike travelling; I don't easily relate to new people or new places. Had God made a mistake in directing me into this ministry?

So often I became intensely conscious of being inadequate for the task. Sometimes, at the end of a tour of meetings, I would become quite distressed, almost depressed, and assailed by a great sense of failure – yet God had manifestly blessed so many people during the tour. Our tour-organisers in each different country saw me as strong, and would have been amazed if I had complained of how weak I felt.

Can we return to 2008 – my 'annus horribilis' as far as physical weakness has been concerned?

During July, smitten by a horrible bug that settled down in my lungs, I received from a dear friend, who regularly collects for me second-hand copies of any of the books by Lilias Trotter, another copy of *Parables of the Christ-Life*. I first read this book back in 1951, before I ever went to the mission field. Lilias Trotter was an amazing woman of the late 1800s, who went as a missionary to North Africa to the Berber people. Not only had she a deep love for the Saviour and a passionate desire to share Him with these desperately needy Muslim people, but she also had a very precious gift – she was a brilliant artist. She could see things in the desert sands that others of us simply never saw. And she put together these two gifts by writing two books, full of exquisite illustrations: *Parables of the Cross* and *Parables of the Christ-life*, where she used the life-cycle of simple plants to illustrate the deep truths of our spiritual lives. I have read the first of these two books many times. I almost know it by heart. But the second book I know less well.

So I re-read *Parables of the Christ-life* last month as I struggled with this chest infection and bodily weakness. And my heart was blessed. Miss Trotter brings out so clearly that in the plant, the new life in the seed, hidden in the seed-case, can only come about by the death of the flower … leaves … every part other than the developing fruit. Likewise, the spiritual life that God gives us at our new birth can only grow and increase as we allow the old life to die. No amount of effort on our part can bring about strength to replace our weakness; only the death-knell to our weakness and its replacement with His strength.

It seems so obvious!

'*My Grace is sufficient for you,*
for My power (strength) is made perfect in weakness.'
Therefore I will boast all the more gladly about my weaknesses,
so that Christ's power (strength) may rest on me.
That is why, for Christ's sake I delight in weaknesses,
In insults, in persecutions, in difficulties.
For when I am weak, then I am strong.'
2 Cor 12:9,10.

May I have truly grasped the principle here – that it is His strength that is to replace my weakness, and not my effort to seek to be strong in my own strength, but to acknowledge that in myself I am weak, but He is willing to replace my weakness with His strength in every instance. My strong sense of being independent, able to cope, not needing the help of others, are all an effort on my part to be what I believed God wanted me to be. Now I have to accept that being dependent on others, allowing them to know they are needed (some honestly seem to see this as a privilege), however weak this may seem in human reasoning, it is actually being strong in the grace of God.

Dr Helen Roseveare was born in England in 1925, brought to faith in Jesus in her first year at University, qualified as a medical doctor in Cambridge in 1950, joined WEC International and sailed for Congo (today, D. R. Congo) in 1953, where she served for 20 years, establishing a medical service and training national paramedical workers. Home to the UK in 1973, Helen has worked as a deputation speaker for WEC worldwide for over 30 years now, as well as writing several books (see below).

Note

1. Books by Lilias Trotter may be procurable from Arab World Ministries, PO Box 51, Loughborough, Leics. LE11 0ZQ

2. Many of the incidents written about in this chapter have been previously recorded, often in greater detail, in one of Helen Roseveare's other books, seven of which are available now from Christian Focus Publications.

Give me this mountain
He gave us a valley
Digging Ditches
Living Sacrifice
Living Faith

Strength out of Weakness

Living Holiness
Living Fellowship

For discussion

A passage to study: 2 Corinthians 11:1 – 12:10

1. Do you see yourself as 'strong' or 'weak'? Is being strong a weakness? Is being weak a strength?

2. What does it mean to 'delight in weakness'? Suggest examples.

3. Review the setbacks, weaknesses and difficulties of your own life at the moment. Does this chapter help you see them differently? In what ways?

Freedom from misplaced loyalty

Patrick Johnstone

Introduction

God's design for me is to be a fitting temple for the Holy Spirit. He patiently works at constructing the building that is me. My life continues to be a building site, for the construction is not yet complete! To take the analogy further my building site is not a 'greenfield' one – a fresh start on an unspoilt piece of new ground. There was an old building there – the old me. It is also an archaeological site. God has to do so much dismantling of the old and sifting through the past in order for my building to be more truly His dwelling.

The new building

In January 1990 I had reached a high point in my ministry life.

The Lord wonderfully brought me to Himself while at Bristol University in England in 1959, and then shortly thereafter called me to minister in the slum townships of Southern Africa with the Dorothea Mission. In 1962 I left for Africa. The 17 years overseas that followed were tough, but fruitful far beyond anything I could have dreamt of. I became a team leader in Zimbabwe (then Rhodesia) and was able to prepare those I led for leadership themselves. I also became a Bible translator (into the Nambya language) and author, compiling early editions of *Operation World* from 1964. This opened doors to wider ministry with OM on the MV Logos in 1979; with WEC as part of the International Office and Director for Research; and into a global role with the Lausanne Movement and the AD2000 and Beyond Movement. By that time around 1.5 million copies of *Operation World* in some 15 languages were in circulation. I had become 'famous' and even in the eyes of many, 'successful'.

In my WEC world, we had launched our STEP advance in 1984 which I had helped to spearhead and orchestrate, leading to significant growth and advances to unreached peoples. My wife Jill and I had also become Deputy Directors of WEC under Dieter and Renate Kuhl's leadership. These were very special years of fruitfulness.

God had also done wonderful things in my inner life too. Not only had he dealt with my sin in forgiving me and continually cleansing me through Jesus' finished work on Calvary, but he had also dealt with much of the encumbering baggage that had weighed me down before and after I became a Christian. Wrong perceptions, and even the enemy's lies that I believed about myself, God and ministry had to be exposed and surrendered as God revealed His Truth to me.

I could look back at the fact that God had called me to serve Him and this gave me a confidence that overcame my youthful lack of it. It also gave me the determination to be true to His calling in spite of difficulties and crises. It steeled me, and also later, Jill, never to leave the place of God's appointment for a negative reason and without an equally clear calling from God to something else.

He had freed me from the deep sense of lack of personal worth which came through years of bullying at school – I was both of Irish descent with a temper to match and also only around five feet tall on my 16th birthday, so very much delayed in physical development. It made me feel I could never attain anything in life, and determined just to keep my head down and out of trouble. I had no idea what I could do with my life, and did not even want to think about it. The death of my father shortly after I had left school with just one barely-passed 'A' level subject forced me to get serious about my future – and about a relationship with God which I did not know I needed!

Freedom from this low self-image became mine in 1964 in Africa. It came from a revelation of Jesus to me as my Life, my Indweller, my Sufficiency through both the Scriptures (especially Revelation 3:16-20) and the avidly read books of Norman Grubb. I never knew that one day I would be invited to join Norman's mission, WEC, and even to get to know him as a friend in his latter years. The great truth became real to me that from now on I could live by the indwelling Lord Jesus, and not strive to live for Him. It no longer mattered what people thought of me; it was Jesus who thought so highly of me that He gave me everything in Himself.

God had also opened my eyes to my spiritual poverty, self-effort and need to be filled with His Holy Spirit for effective ministry. Instead of struggle, service became more of a resting in His work through me, and with an expectation He would give whatever gifts I needed for any task He gave me. What a release! All became possible if He was leading.

Yet there were warning signs of another area of de-construction that was needed. In 1982-4 I went through a time of mild burn-out, which played havoc with my sleep patterns and efficiency in work. We had spent six very busy years without a break, in Africa and then on the high seas with the MV Logos. During the last year on the ship I would fall asleep any time I sat still. My body was telling me to stop and rest, but my desire to fulfil the expectations of others pushed me on – how could I let them down? We came to our new job at Bulstrode, the WEC UK headquarters, after just one month of holiday – over Christmas and New Year, so hardly restful. Then came the steep learning curve of absorbing a new mission culture and complex organization as a new leader. In 1982 I came to a crisis when my body changed its tune, and instead of demanding it, my body denied me sleep, and for weeks I slept hardly at all. I had made a basic unwritten rule for myself of only saying 'No' to any invitation or task where I already had a prior engagement. In fact I was a compulsive volunteer! I could not do it all, for I did not have the hours in the day to satisfy every demand made on me by others! However it took another 20 years to understand why I did this and find a measure of freedom in this area of compulsive volunteerism or over-commitment to loyalty.

A new dismantling

In that month, January 1990, came the first warning from the Lord. I was contemplating God's goodness to me. I was deeply happy in ministry and in a fulfilling marriage with Jill with three offspring who were all committed to the Lord Jesus. Then the Lord whispered in my heart that a deep trial awaited me in the year ahead. I well remember the icy cold feeling that came over me. I could only wonder what that might possibly be.

In June that year we gathered for a Johnstone family reunion near Gloucester at my sister's farm. We played tennis, and Jill picked up a racquet to hit a ball but almost immediately felt excruciating pain in her back. After several months, it had only become worse, so we went along to our GP. I was insistent on going with her because we had had poor experiences with this doctor for casually assuming that anyone living in the large, crowded WEC Bulstrode community must be suffering from psycho-somatic disorders. He heeded my insistence that all Jill's symptoms be examined properly. He took action and within a few days we had the shocking news that Jill had a pathological break of her spine. It took several months before they could eventually diagnose that it was a secondary cancer. God gave her and us much grace over the next two years before, in June 1994, Jill died. She almost completed her children's version of *Operation World*, and blessed many people with her faith and fortitude over that time. I threw myself back into the labour of completing the next edition of *Operation World* which was published the following year and also into my ministry in WEC and in international travel and ministry.

Jill and I had grown up in our Christian experience and ministry in the Dorothea Mission. The mission was passionately committed to prayer and evangelism, but there was an unwritten code of loyalty to the Mission as the highest attribute of a worker. Both of us imbibed this cultural value, and unwittingly were hurting each other and those near and dear to us by this compulsive volunteerism! Now I had lost my Jill.

After Jill's death I was determined to press on, expecting my relationship with Jesus to more than make up her loss. I had not reckoned on the matchmakers and self-considered suitable marriage partners that began to attach themselves to me. I realized I would have to reconsider my position on marriage. This is what ultimately opened me up to the possibility of marriage, and then to me marrying Robyn in 1995, Jill's former co-worker between 1990 and 1992. That, in itself is another amazing story! Robyn had not had the same baptism into Dorothea Mission loyalty, but came with her own unresolved life baggage. So actually living with express-train Patrick with his issues of compulsive volunteerism was traumatic. Neither of us could fully understand the issues involved, and it took years for us to find a measure of understanding of the wrong worldviews and lies of the enemy that underlay the stresses we went through. However we both found our needed freedoms and present richness in our marriage relationship.

The deconstruction process was well under way, but to better explain I need to do some 'archaeology'!

The old building's archaeology

When I dug into my family history I began to understand why I was as I was. My father's side of the family were Irish with roots in Co. Cavan, but of Scottish Ulster Settlement stock. My grandfather moved to England around 1899, buying a medical practice in N.

Gloucestershire. Popop, as we called him, was devoted to his wife Weeshie. She must have been a lovely person – she was the goddaughter of Mrs Alexander, the writer of many favourite hymns such as 'All things bright and beautiful' and 'There is a green hill far away'. Weeshie had four children, two girls followed by two boys, but in 1918 when my father, the first son, was 11, Weeshie died after a miscarriage was poorly handled by a doctor colleague. Popop was distraught and the family was devastated. The ripple effects of this unexpected tragedy deeply affect our family up to today. My grandfather never re-married and mourned Weeshie's death until he died 40 years later. In his grief he took morphine, and became addicted to it and was even registered as an addict.

The effect on my father and uncle was enormous. My father Peter (Maxwell) was the special one for my grandfather as my uncle Hec (Desmond) was the special one for my grandmother. When time came for university there was only sufficient money to send Peter to Cambridge to study medicine. Hec wanted to go too, but had to join the army, where he saved money earned through the War to put himself through medical school. He was a driven man, who made good and eventually succeeded at great personal cost.

My father was successful in his studies and then as an anaesthetist at St Thomas's Hospital in London. Yet he carried the weight of knowledge that he had been favoured to get the education denied to his brother. This became a weight of responsibility and loyalty from which he could not escape. In 1936 came the summons from my grandfather to come back to the country GP practice to help him – also in administering the morphine he needed. My father reluctantly went, but he hated the move and the job of being a GP in a poor pre-National Health Service practice. This led to deep depression, severe stomach ulcers, operations and weakness. It ultimately contributed to his early death by drowning (he tried to do more than for what he had strength) when we were on holiday in Cornwall in 1957. In one sense his ill-health and death could be attributed to his high degree of obligation and loyalty. The same values had been absorbed by me too, and I had not realized it. They had then been reinforced through my years in the Dorothea Mission in Africa.

The death of my grandmother had many outworkings over succeeding generations too. It impacted my parents' marriage, for my father was then living in his father's house, and my mother had a very hard time as a young foreigner (she was Dutch) having to take over a big household not her own, that had not had a woman's influence for 20 years, and later with my father deeply unhappy and increasingly depressed. I admire her courage.

It also affected my brother and I. I was the eldest, and I remember well my early childhood in which my father gave me much time as a little boy – we studied maps together, laying the foundations of a lasting interest in geography and the writing of *Operation World*. He stimulated me to be curious. He taught me the names of birds, trees and mushrooms, and how to play chess, tennis and squash. My brother was four years younger than me, but by the time he had reached an age when my father could do the same for him, my father was in depression and could give him little time. I now see, in retrospect, how damaging this was to my brother, Rob. There was the constant cry for attention and help manifested in many ways – and later in life a drive for perfection that ultimately drove him to manic depression and eventually to him committing suicide. Our own relationship was always good, but he always felt so inferior to me even though I was a miserable failure at school, and he a brilliant success. I had to speak at his funeral – one of the saddest days of my life. I learnt from this how important our past is in understanding distorted world-views that cripple so many in Christian service – serving with issues still not admitted or even understood.

A new extension

Robyn came to us as gift of God in answer to prayer! Jill did much to keep our office functioning and provided the essential hub for communication for us in the International Office. It was only after she had gone did we fully appreciate what we had lost. It certainly slowed and limited my ministry output. In her busy life with also caring for family and my frequent absences overseas, she had little time to put into action a long-held desire to write a children's version of *Operation World*. She needed a co-worker who could take on the basics of running the research office. We could not offer a salary, so this person had to be a volunteer – not easy to find!

Jill and I decided to set aside a day for fasting and prayer. So we spent the morning to mid-afternoon in our Bulstrode flat praying specifically for this one need. In the middle of the afternoon, the phone rang, and on answering it found myself speaking to a Californian. Robyn wanted to know if we had a place for her to work with *Operation World* – since the Lord had touched her heart in this direction after using the book to stimulate prayer in her local church. I gulped, had a huge lump in my throat, but tried not to sound too emotional at this dramatic and immediate answer to prayer. So I think I communicated to this lady a very matter-of-fact set of responses in spite of the fact I was overcome with emotion! A British stiff upper lip? I recommended that she come through applying to WEC USA. This she did, and she became one of the fastest recruits ever processed from the point of application to arrival on the field! Within a year she was with us and working with Jill. Her coming made Jill's book *You Can Change the World* possible and was a great boost for the information processing for the emerging new edition of *Operation World*.

Some time after Jill's death, Robyn left us to prepare to go to Bulgaria for ministry among the Turkish-speaking population of that newly opened land. She eventually went to Turkey for a year to learn Turkish. Little did I know that many people early on had suspected or discerned that Robyn and I would eventually marry. Robyn played a piece of music on her flute at Jill's funeral. And a Christian friend leaned over to her husband and commented that Robyn would be Patrick's wife one day. My thoughts were far from that for a long time. These friends only shared what they had discussed after we were engaged! My son Tim and daughter Ruth had long awaited such a development, because they did not know of anyone else within WEC that would suit me. Hearing later of these revelations to others was a comfort for us both that God was in it even if there were tough years ahead!

When Robyn was in Turkey I felt it right to write to her asking about the possibility of a relationship which might involve marriage. Then everything happened almost too quickly for both of us. With daily phone calls over a week it ended up with more than a relationship and it became an engagement. In retrospect we should have slowed things down a bit, because my diary for 18 months ahead was fairly full and we therefore did not have the biblical year to enjoy life together without too many external pressures. I did not fully realize the impact this would have on Robyn. Yet, in God's grace, it all ultimately worked to a deeper freedom for both of us from the encumbering baggage we had brought, unwittingly, into our marriage. We certainly would not have discovered this before marrying, for we needed the shock and pain to begin seeking God's remedy in Jesus.

We married in February 1995 at our USA HQ and after a honeymoon in New Zealand went on to an intense five-week tour of Australia – with two or three meetings daily and travel between states on our 'off' days. It gained the nickname from Robyn, 'The Tour from Hell'. It was traumatic for her and certainly coloured our own relationship for years thereafter. It was hard for her to share about this pain – how could she criticize this famous person she had married whose ministry was so widely acclaimed, and who seemed so 'nice'?

Robyn's pain set her on a voyage of searching and eventually discovering her baggage of paternal rejection and lack of love, and then finding a new and intimate relationship with her Heavenly Father. For this to happen I had to address my issue of misplaced loyalty that had pushed Robyn into such pain with my compulsive ability to say 'Yes'. I first had to realize it and then confess it to the Lord and her, but that process took years. My confession freed up Robyn to make her own journey to freedom.

We are both still learning. Robyn still feels that I have not completely been freed from the excess of misplaced loyalty, and desire to please people. In many ways this particular trait can be a blessing and asset, but my loyalty to God must be paramount, and only doing what I hear Him doing, and speaking what I hear Him speaking. I want to be found pleasing Him and not just people. May I continue to learn – even if it is like peeling layers of an onion. Yet from all we have learnt, it is leading us into a wider ministry of ministering to other Christian workers. So many have been ministering for much of their lives, but still have not found freedoms that Jesus has offered us all to enjoy. The words of Jesus are so meaningful: 'If the Son shall make you free, you shall be free indeed'!

Robyn is now nearly two years into a very good on-line post-graduate degree course on Spiritual Formation which has much to do with member care, mentoring, and giving spiritual encouragement to Christian workers. She is passionate for people to know God's transforming power and enjoy the liberty there is in Jesus. It is likely that her ministry will develop further in this direction in and beyond WEC. I admire the grace and power of God in her life, and the enrichment that has come to both of us. I see this as all fruit of the journey through which God has brought us both – separately and together. I suppose my big question is, 'Oh Lord, why does it take me so long to learn?'!

Patrick Johnstone is the founding author of the best-selling prayer handbook Operation World and the popular The Church Is Bigger Than You Think. Along with his first wife Jill, Patrick served both as Research Director and Deputy International Director of WEC International.

For discussion

1. Reflect on this idea of 'compulsive volunteerism' or 'misplaced loyalty'.

Freedom from misplaced loyalty

What is the difference between a godly self-denial and 'compulsive volunteerism'

Can loyalty be misplaced or overdone? Do you recognize the symptoms in your own life?

2. Patrick Johnstone writes about 'only doing what I see Jesus doing and only speaking what I hear him speaking' which is a reference to John 8:28-30. What does this mean? How does this work out in everyday life? (See also John 6:25-59 which tells us 'Do not work for food that spoils, but for food that endures to eternal life' (v. 27).)

3. Patrick tells about a day of prayer and fasting which results in a dramatic answered prayer. Have you thought of setting aside a day and skipping a couple of meals to focus on seeking God?

Secure in God's love

Daphne Spraggett

'A missionary! Oh, how wonderful!' enthused the woman who had come to teach the long-term patients in the children's ward in the Mildmay Mission Hospital in London. I cringed. At that moment, being a missionary was proving both painful and traumatic, and yet ... My little daughter Jenny, not yet two years old, was in the cubicle next to mine in that children's ward and Roy, my husband, was in another ward in that same London hospital.

What had happened and why we were in hospital? Why had God allowed it all to happen? Why hadn't God kept us safe? Hadn't we been sure of the promise in Psalm 91:11 'For he will command his angels concerning you to guard you in all your ways'? Hadn't we committed each day to Him? Had He forsaken us?

A few weeks earlier we had been living and working among both tribal and Vietnamese people in an area not far from the demilitarized zone between South and North Vietnam. We were only too aware that the infiltration and activities of the Viet Cong (communist) guerrillas in the area were intensifying rapidly. They had already abducted three tribal Christians, planted mines along some of the trails into the villages and were determined to get rid of those they considered American spies. So it was that one night in January 1964 these guerrillas planted a bomb on the side of our house, blowing the house to pieces. We were certainly not meant to get out of it alive. However, local people dug us out of the rubble and cared for us through the night; when daylight came an American Army ambulance rescued us. American doctors and nurses gave us emergency surgery in one of their field hospitals. We were then transferred to a private hospital until we could make the long, painful flight back to England. What did the future hold? It seemed our own ministry in Vietnam had come to an end: yes, we were all alive but we'd lost more or less everything we possessed, the future was uncertain, and I was concerned for the baby I was expecting.

It was a traumatic experience, and yet ... And yet through it all was an amazing sense of the love of God surrounding us, embracing us and holding us tight. There in that hospital ward in London, God ministered to me through His word. Quietly there came the assurance of His faithfulness and love, and then the overwhelming truth of Romans 8:31-39 burst on my heart and mind. Nothing can ever separate us from the love of God that is in Christ Jesus our Lord. Nothing!

It was one of those important, confirming experiences in my life. I realised afresh the immensity and power as well as the depth and intimacy of His steadfast, never-failing love.

Years earlier, as a small child, I'd first become aware of the love of God. Sunday School was the highlight of my week! There, through godly teachers, I learnt of the Saviour Jesus who was sent by God and died on the cross for my sin. Even though I couldn't see Him, and couldn't express it, I knew God loved me! He loved me even more than did my loving, caring parents. Often, as we huddled together in air raid shelters during World War II, we were reminded that whatever happened we were safe in God's love and care. God's word tells us:

Secure in God's love

'God is love. Whoever lives in love lives in God, and God in him. In this way, love is made complete among us ... There is no fear in love. But perfect love drives out fear, because fear has to do with punishment. (1 John 4:16b-18).

That awareness of God's love was always there in the background of my life and a number of years later, while I was training as a teacher, what God had done for me through Jesus' death on the cross became reality to me in a new way. Incredible to know that 'God made him who had no sin to be sin for us, so that in him we might become the righteousness of God' (2 Cor. 5:21). How great is His love!

Another thing I learnt from my Sunday school teachers was that God loved the boys and girls in other lands, too, and that Jesus died for their sins as well as for mine. Our teachers emphasised that so great was His love that He wanted everyone everywhere to know that love for themselves. They told us stories of missionaries who had spent their lives in dark and difficult places to tell others of God's great love and had, themselves, even in extremely hard circumstances, experienced the truth that nothing could 'ever separate them from the love of God that is in Christ Jesus our Lord'. Young as I was, I decided in my heart that I, too, would become a missionary.

As I look back over my life, memories of times when I've experienced that steadfast, unchanging love of God have come flooding back. Sometimes it has come through the kindness of others, sometimes through circumstances, sometimes through what has seemed a direct intervention or provision from God.

How often the unexpected kindness of others has portrayed God's love! Who would expect the Principal of the Missionary Training College in Glasgow to be concerned that a student hadn't, perhaps, enough money to buy a cup of tea on the overnight coach journey home at the end of term? How did he know that I had little more in my purse than my fare across London from one bus station to another? As he put a few coins in my hand, I was overwhelmed by the assurance of God's love. What about the dear, elderly lady who for 24 years wrote every month with a gift from her own scanty resources? There were the Christian nurses and doctors who sat with me and helped me with far more than medical care during those long months in hospital. Later, a businessman decided that we needed a reliable car for our work in Scotland and provided us with one, changing it every few years, for more than 30 years. How often we saw God's love expressed through the kindness of others. How often we were blessed through them. And how often we realised afresh His unfailing love in every circumstance of life.

God doesn't forsake us when the way is hard or when we have difficult decisions to make or even when we make a hash of things. What a blessing to know that in His love for us, Christ Jesus is there at the right hand of God interceding for us and that He will meet with us and show us the way to go.

When we came home from Vietnam, we certainly didn't know the way ahead and found it difficult to pray. Then we were invited to join the staff at the Glasgow Missionary Training College for a period. Surrounded there by God's loving, caring people, it proved a time of healing for body, mind and heart. But we needed to know His will for our future service. We certainly knew He hadn't abandoned us and would not turn His back on us. As we waited on God, and as the staff prayed too, there came the conviction that we should stay on at the College. Time and again through the years as we faced fresh challenges or a change of direction, it was with the assurance that God already knew the way ahead and had His own plan for us.

More recently, having lived at WEC's headquarters, Bulstrode, for 13 years, I knew the time had come to move out and needed to know where to live. But where? One day, as I passed some flats near my daughter's home, it seemed as if God was telling me that this was the place He had prepared for me. So, in many ways, it was no surprise when Alison phoned to ask if I would be interested in one of the flats. God, in His love, had already spoken.

Secure in God's love

God is there with us, too, when the way is tough. We are never promised in Scripture that being a Christian means life will be smooth and easy. On the contrary, there are many references to the hardship and difficulties that will be encountered as we walk with Him. But what glorious promises there are that He is faithful and will be with us in all that we face! Throughout the centuries, Christians have proved this and experienced His presence time and again. They experienced it in New Testament times as we read in Acts; all round the world, Christians are still experiencing it today as they suffer persecution for His Name's sake. How many are assured by Paul's words in Romans 8:28-29:

> We know that in all things God works for the good of those who love him, who have been called according to his purpose. For those God foreknew he also predestined to be conformed to the likeness of his Son ...

'Conformed to the image of His Son'! God has His purposes in all that happens to us and we can be sure that in all we encounter that nothing 'will be able to separate us from the love of God that is in Christ Jesus our Lord' for He is conforming us to the image of His Son.

Some years ago, Roy and I went through a very difficult and painful experience which affected every part of our lives and ministry. Had God abandoned us? It felt like it. All our past experiences and dependence on His promises told us that He had not, but there was conflict in our minds and hearts. Where was He? One rainy day, as we wept and prayed, I asked Him for a sign, a rainbow perhaps, to give us the assurance of His continued love and care. I lifted my head. God gave far more than a rainbow. On that wet, gray day, when the dark clouds seemed to press in on us, a brilliant shaft of sunlight shone right into the room. There was only a tiny break in the clouds, but it was enough for that ray of sunshine and the assurance of God's love to reach us. Our prayers turned to praise! How great is His unfailing love!

Life Lessons

It was such a personal message to us. God's unfailing love is so intimate. He is concerned with me as an individual. He knows all about me. He knows the way in which I need His love demonstrated at any given time. He knows when that love needs to come to me as a hug; He knows, too, when it needs to come as a word of encouragement, a word of assurance, a word of guidance or even a word of reproof and forgiveness. God's love is not a general, wishy-washy experience but strong and powerful, far beyond our comprehension.

The immensity and intimacy of His love touched my heart again while I was working on some research. As I read through reports and statistics, my heart welled with wonder and praise. All round the world are millions of people who know that same personal intimacy with the Lord that I know; in His great love He has the same concern for each individual as He has for me; Christ intercedes for each one just as He does for me; and our Heavenly Father listens to the prayers and cries of everyone. How great He is!

When God called Roy 'Home', suddenly and unexpectedly, one morning in December 1999, once again came the assurance that even in this experience nothing is 'able to separate us from the love of God that is in Christ Jesus our Lord.' Once again, there was His own intimate embrace holding me tight. He knew my need and I thank God for my precious daughters and their families as we shared our memories and God's love together. I thank Him, too, for each friend who helped me through that time. Once more, God's steadfast love was being expressed through others. Then, in His intimate love, He ministered through His word, through the reading of Scripture, through sermons, through verses written in cards. One special one was

May our Lord Jesus Christ himself and God our Father, who loved us and by his grace gave us eternal encouragement and good hope, encourage your hearts and strengthen you in every good deed and word (2 Thessalonians 2:16-17).

Secure in God's love

I needed that! Eternal encouragement and good hope, a gift of God! Another which blesses me each day says 'May the God of hope fill you with all joy and peace as you trust in him, so that you may overflow with hope by the power of the Holy Spirit' (Romans 15:13) – not just with a trickle but with an overflowing of hope. To me both verses give that focus of reaching out with His love to others who also need the assurance of His steadfast love as they pass through difficult times.

As day follows day I become more aware of God's steadfast love for me and for all His family everywhere. Our experiences are all different, but God meets each one as we have need. By His grace, my desire is that I may ever seek to live with that full assurance and conviction that

Nothing can ever separate us from God's love. Neither death nor life, neither angels nor demons, neither our fears for today nor our worries about tomorrow – not even the powers of hell can separate us from God's love. No power in the sky above or in the earth below – indeed, nothing in all creation will ever be able to separate us from the love of God that is revealed in Christ Jesus our Lord (Romans 8:38-39 NLT).

Daphne Spraggett served with her husband Roy in Vietnam from 1959-1964. They subsequently worked in various WEC roles, including teaching at aWEC training college and serving as Regional Directors for the South Asian region.

Along with Jill Johnstone, Daphne worked on the children's prayer guides

You can change the world (1991)
You too can change the world (1996)
Window on the world (2001)

Life Lessons

For discussion

'As I look back over my life, memories of times when I've experienced that steadfast, unchanging love of God have come flooding back. Sometimes it has come through the kindness of others, sometimes through circumstances, sometimes through what has seemed a direct intervention or provision from God.'

1. Get each person in the group to tell something of their story, as Daphne has , pointing out personal experiences of the love of God.

2. Spend time worshipping God together.

WEC International

WEC International is a missions agency with over 1,800 workers drawn from 50 countries serving in multicultural teams among nearly 90 unreached peoples of the world. From its beginnings in the Congo in 1913 it has grown to work in many different parts of the world. Evangelical and inter-denominational in outlook, WEC's ethos is based on Four Pillars of Faith, Sacrifice, Holiness, and Fellowship. WEC's commission is:

- To bring the gospel of our Lord Jesus Christ to the remaining unevangelised peoples of the world with utmost urgency
- To demonstrate the compassion of Christ to a needy world
- To plant churches and lead them to spiritual maturity
- To inspire, mobilise and train for cross-cultural mission.

To help us achieve that, we have 16 Sending Bases scattered

throughout the world which recruit, screen, send and help support workers. We also train missionary workers at six training institutes around the world.

WEC workers are involved in almost every type of direct outreach and support ministry related to the fulfilment of these aims. WEC's ministries range from producing the prayer handbook *Operation World*, through planting and establishing churches, to encouraging national missionary sending agencies in mature WEC fields.

Our Lifestyle

- We fervently desire to see Christ formed in us so that we live holy lives.
- In dependence on the Holy Spirit we determine to obey our Lord whatever the cost.
- We trust God completely to meet every need and challenge we face in His service.
- We are committed to oneness, fellowship and the care of our whole missionary family.

Our Convictions

- We are convinced that prayer is a priority.
- We uphold biblical truth and standards.
- We affirm our love for Christ's Church, and endeavour to work in fellowship with local and national churches, and with other Christian agencies.
- We accept each other irrespective of gender, ethnic background or church affiliation.
- We desire to work in multi-national teams and are committed to effective international cooperation.
- We recognise the importance of research and responding to God's directions for advance.

WEC International

- We believe in full participation and oneness in decision making.
- We value servant leaders who wait on God for vision and direction.
- We promote local and innovative strategies through decentralised decision making.
- We make no appeals for funds.

'If Jesus Christ be God and died for me, no sacrifice can be too great for me to make for Him.'
C T Studd

www.wec-int.org

Christian Focus Publications

publishes books for all ages

Our mission statement –

STAYING FAITHFUL

In dependence upon God we seek to help make His infallible Word, the Bible, relevant. Our aim is to ensure that the Lord Jesus Christ is presented as the only hope to obtain forgiveness of sin, live a useful life and look forward to heaven with Him.

REACHING OUT

Christ's last command requires us to reach out to our world with His gospel. We seek to help fulfil that by publishing books that point people towards Jesus and help them develop a Christ-like maturity. We aim to equip all levels of readers for life, work, ministry and mission.

Books in our adult range are published in three imprints.

Christian Focus contains popular works including biographies, commentaries, basic doctrine and Christian living. Our children's books are also published in this imprint.

Mentor focuses on books written at a level suitable for Bible College and seminary students, pastors, and other serious readers. The imprint includes commentaries, doctrinal studies, examination of current issues and church history.

Christian Heritage contains classic writings from the past.

Christian Focus Publications, Ltd
Geanies House, Fearn,
Ross-shire, IV20 1TW, Scotland, United Kingdom
info@christianfocus.com

Our titles are available from quality bookstores and
www.christianfocus.com